Bible Pathway

BIBLICAL FUNDAMENTALS OF

PRAYER

Presented to

_____

_____

_____

_____

_____

_____

_____

By

_____

Date

_____

BIBLE PATHWAY

BIBLICAL FUNDAMENTALS OF

PRAYER

JOHN A. HASH

DD., Litt.D

Published By

BIBLE PATHWAY MINISTRIES

INTERNATIONAL

P. O. Box 20123
Murfreesboro, Tennessee 37129

Acknowledgements

I ESPECIALLY WANT TO THANK Barbara Bivens, Sue Cawthron, Rita Guerra, Karen Hawkins, Kenneth Roy Roberts III, Ken Sharp, and Benjamin Wallace for their invaluable contributions in researching and editing this book.

Recognition

LOVING RECOGNITION IS EXTENDED TO my wife, Letha, who has been an encouragement to me for over 60 years. Her spiritual insight, patience, and advice have been priceless, and I admire her with great esteem.

John A Hash

John A. Hash

The King James Version of the Bible is used as the basis for all quotations. Any portion of this book may be reprinted with permission by adding the following credit line: "Reprinted from *Bible Pathway Biblical Fundamentals of Prayer*, by John A. Hash; Bible Pathway Ministries; Murfreesboro, Tennessee."

Index Pages for Chapters

FOREWORD

Know what you believe. Know why you believe it. Then live it!

That's the theme of every Greek and Hebrew language class I've ever taught. It is also the theme of one man whose ministry stands tall among those who are raised up by God to advance His Kingdom.

More than half a century ago, Dr. John Hash first grasped what should be to all of us the obvious connection between reading Scripture and knowing how to pray. Unless you know what the Bible says, you cannot know what you believe. And unless you know what you believe, you cannot be committed to living it.

This book represents the wisdom Dr. Hash has gained through his years of repeated study of God's Word. You will receive remarkable direction as you seek to pray in harmony with scriptural truths.

From the outset, you will see how the prayers of Genesis tie to the prayers of the New Testament. You will recognize how each chapter fits into the whole of God's revelation, and you will understand the impact of the prayers in each biblical account on the people involved. Consequently, you will better understand how it applies to your own prayer life.

Since the focus of *The Biblical Fundamentals of*

Prayer is Scripture itself, each chapter is relevant to one or more biblical principles of answered prayer.

There may be chapters when the clarity of a particular truth sets you on the mountaintop. Yet there may be other chapters when God communicates His direction gradually over several days, or maybe even weeks. But be assured that He does have a message for you, and you will hear Him speak it in a way that you will understand. Your part is to be faithful in reading His Book, *that you might be filled with the knowledge of His will in all wisdom and spiritual understanding; that you might walk worthy of the Lord to all pleasing, being fruitful in every good work, and increasing in the knowledge of God; strengthened with all might, according to His glorious power, to all patience and long-suffering with joyfulness; giving thanks to the Father, which has made us meet to be partakers of the inheritance of the saints in light* (Colossians 1:9-12).

– Samuel J. Gantt, III
Former Director of Biblical Language Instruction,
Fuller Theological Seminary, Pasadena, California

PREFACE

The supreme reason for living is to please our Creator. Pity the person who is wasting the few short years of life chasing earthly goals to obtain financial security, popularity, or material success, but failing to achieve the purpose for which God created them!

God has allotted just one short lifetime:

1. To know the One True God. There is only One Living God who is a Trinity expressed in three Persons: *The Father . . . the Son* (Jesus born in Bethlehem), *and . . . the Holy Spirit* (Genesis 28:18-20), Who dwells within every Christian. All other gods are false, lifeless counterfeits that can save no one from eternal hell fire, where there is *weeping and gnashing of teeth* forever (22:13). They cannot answer our prayers or provide for our needs. *For there is One God, and One Mediator between God and men, the Man Christ Jesus* (I Timothy 2:5; also John 14:16-17; 16:13-15; I John 5:7).

2. To learn, through reading the Word of God, how to pray. God has said that *the Holy Scriptures* (the Old Testament) *are able to make you wise to salvation through faith which is in Christ Jesus. All Scripture is given by inspiration of God, and is profitable for doctrine, for reproof, for correction, for instruction in righteousness* (in holy living, in conformity to God's will in thought, purpose, and action)*: That the man of God may be perfect* (adequate)*, thoroughly furnished* (efficient, well prepared) *to all good works*

8

(II Timothy 3:15-17).

3. To be prepared to face eternity. Jesus said: *Man shall not live by bread alone, but by **every Word** that proceeds out of the mouth of God* (Matthew 4:4). ***Bread*** refers to our daily food; but, ***every Word** that proceeds out of the mouth of God* is important to accomplish the purposes for which God created us. ***Every Word*** begins with Genesis 1:1 and ends with Revelation 22:21. If we fail to read ***all Scripture*** (the Bible), we will miss out on some of the things God wants us to know in order to pray effectively.

4. To share this message with others. Jesus says: ***Go ... teach all nations ... to observe ALL THINGS I have commanded you*** (Matthew 28:19-20).

Everyone believes that God hears their prayers; but we need to take God seriously when He says: *He that turns away his ear from hearing the Law* (the Word of God), *even his prayer shall be abomination* (Proverbs 28:9).

I pray as I write each chapter *that you might be filled with the knowledge of His will in all wisdom and spiritual understanding; That you might walk worthy of the Lord to all pleasing, being fruitful in every good work, and increasing in the knowledge of God* (Colossians 1:9-10; also II Peter 3:18).

– John A. Hash, D.D., Litt.D.,
Founder & Editor in Chief
Bible Pathway Ministries International

We all have sinned against the Lord
And stand condemned by His own Word,
No prayer or plea of ours could win
God's free forgiveness for all sin

But Jesus came and took our place
That He might save us by His grace;
He bore our sins — so great and wide —
That we, through Him, be justified.

And as we plead Christ's work complete
Upon the Cross — where He did meet
Each claim of God's most righteous Law —
God wipes away each sin and flaw.

He speaks His peace within the heart
And bids all guilt and fear depart,
Counts, us accepted in His Son
And sees the life of faith begun.

May we, in gratitude and love,
Seek ever those things that are Above
And let Christ live His life anew
Through all who love His will to do.

M.E. Harding

Introduction

The importance of prayer in a Christian's life cannot be emphasized enough.

In His **"How-To-Pray Manual," the Holy Bible**, God has provided answers to every prayer need of the human heart by recording more than 250 individual prayers of the prophets, kings, and apostles, as well as the Lord Himself. It is a wonderful fact that our loving Heavenly Father has chosen to communicate with us as His children. From these prayers and the people who prayed them we learn how to pray and live to be assured of answers from God. Thus, it is of utmost importance that we read all the Bible from Genesis through Revelation. To think we can ignore any of it is to question the purposes of God, who said: *All Scripture is inspired of God, and is profitable* (II Timothy 3:16). If it is *all profitable* and we do not read all of it, then we fail to gain **the best preparation for prayer** that God has planned for us.

Nothing is more satisfying than to prayerfully read His Word, He is speaking directly to us. And, as we pray, we are speaking directly to our Heavenly Father, who listens to us. By doing this, we experience true fellowship with our unseen Holy Heavenly Father.

When manufacturers produce new equipment, they include instruction manuals to enable the consumer to gain the maximum benefit from their product. And the more complicated the equipment, the more instruction is given. Similarly, the Triune God – God the Father, God the Son, and God the Holy Spirit – has provided just one all-inclusive **"manual of instruction"** for His children **to teach us how to pray effectively and how to live successfully**. It is very detailed and was written by about 40 men in 66 books over a period of 1500 years to illustrate every possible qualification and every hindrance to prayer. He had it all recorded in His only infallible prayer manual. Most of the writers never knew one another, yet all the books in the Bible are in perfect harmony.

No better "how-to-pray manual" has ever been written than the Bible. Think how tragic it would be to fall short of fulfilling God's perfect will – **wasting our few short years** achieving earthly material, social, and financial goals for self-gratification – but failing to achieve the eternal purpose for which He created us.

Let us come to the Scriptures reverently, praying *that the God of our Lord Jesus Christ, the Father of glory,* **may give to you the spirit of wisdom** *and revelation in the knowledge of Him: The eyes of your understanding* (mind) *being enlightened; that you may know what is the hope of His calling, and what the riches of the glory of His inheritance in the saints, And what is* **the exceeding greatness of His power to us-ward** (toward us) *who believe, according to the working of His mighty power* (Ephesians 1:17-19). May the dominating motive in all our prayers be *that we might walk worthy of the Lord to all pleasing, being fruitful in every good work, and increasing in the knowledge of God* (Colossians 1:10).

Thought for the day: *The* LORD *is near to all them that call upon* (pray to) *Him, to all that call upon Him in truth. He will fulfill the desire of them that fear Him: He also will hear their cry* (prayer), *and will save them* (Psalm 145:18-19).

Abram

The development of **Abram's faith** began after he and his nephew Lot left Ur of the Chaldees on their journey of about 800 miles to the promised land (see Genesis 11:31; 12:4). *Now the LORD had said to Abram, Get you out of your country, and from your kindred, and from your father's house, to a land that I will show you: And I will make of you a great nation, and I will bless you, and make your name great; and you shall be a blessing* (12:1-2). Upon arriving in Canaan, they encountered a famine. This must have been a great disappointment, so they continued south into Egypt **without praying about it**. There Abram encountered an embarrassing situation and was forced to leave Egypt (see 12:10-20). Abram and Lot returned to Canaan and settled in the south near Sodom where the pastureland was good. Because Abram and Lot both had large flocks, soon *there was a strife* (quarreling) *between the herdsmen of Abram's cattle* (livestock) *and the herdsmen of Lot's cattle* (13:7).

Abram could have taken the best land for himself since he was older than his nephew and was the spiritual leader. Instead, he graciously said to Lot: *Let there be no strife . . . for we are brethren. Is not the whole land before you?* (let us) *separate . . . if you will take the left hand, then I will go to the right* (13:8-9). Lot selfishly took advantage of Abram's generosity and chose **all** the well-watered plain near Sodom. Lot decided to ignore his spiritual need to be in fellowship with Abram. Instead, he made friends with the people of Sodom, who were *wicked and sinners before the* LORD *exceedingly* (13:10-13).

This was a testing of Abram's faith and probably was even a greater disappointment. He could have asked: "Where is the blessing?" And God's promise to make Abram's "name great" seemed even more remote. It probably appeared to him that he was left without anything. However, it was after this encounter with Lot that Abram received another promise from the Lord that He would make Abram's *seed* (descendants) as numerous as *the dust of the earth* (13:16). Then he went north to live *in the plain of Mamre . . . in Hebron, and built there an altar* **(a place of prayer** and sacrifice) *to the* LORD (13:18).

His faith was again tested sometime later when the Lord revealed to Abram that He would destroy

Sodom. Abram could have said: "Lot took advantage of me and now he will get what he deserves." But **Abram began to intercede in prayer for his undeserving nephew**, and Lot was delivered out of the city of Sodom before it was destroyed (see 18:16 – 19:29).

As Jesus did, and as He commanded His people to do, we need to **pray for those who despitefully use us** (see Matthew 5:44). Luke was also inspired to record Jesus' words: *Bless them that curse you, and pray for them which despitefully use you* (Luke 6:28). As followers of Christ, we must do the same if **our prayers are to be answered**.

The person we pray for or help may or may not appreciate or deserve the kindness shown. Our responsibility, however, is not to the person who needs prayer or help but to the Lord, who is the true Owner of all creation and who provides the opportunities for us to express His love.

In contrast to Abram, there is no record that Lot built an altar of sacrifice to worship the Lord and pray while in Sodom – or even after he was delivered from death. He was typical of many Christians today who may deplore our wicked society but who make decisions that greatly affect their lives based solely on personal or material advantages and **without praying for guidance**. They assume that if they don't commit "serious sins," they are free to devote their lives to worldly pursuits **without praying about what God would have them do**. But the few who *seek first the Kingdom of God and His righteousness* (Matthew 6:33) **pray seriously for the fulfillment of their Savior's plan for their lives**. Jesus made it clear that *no servant can serve two masters: for either he will hate the one, and love the other; or else he will hold to the one, and despise the other. You cannot serve God and mammon* (wealth) (Luke 16:13). What we do or fail to do exhibits the choice we have made – either for Christ or self – since there is no neutral position. Satan seeks to plant doubt that, when we pray to serve the Lord, we have chosen the best in life.

As Abram did for Lot, **it is important to intercede in prayer for others** – even when you may believe they are undeserving, or when they have hurt or misused you in some way. *If your brother trespass against you, rebuke him: and if he repent, forgive him. And if he trespasses against you seven times in a day, and seven times in a day turn again to you, saying, I repent: you shall forgive him* (Luke 17:3-4). **Stephen prayed** for those who were stoning him (see Acts 7:59-60). But, our greatest example of intercession is Jesus, who **prayed on the cross for those who were crucifying Him**. He prayed: *Father, forgive them; for they know not what they do* (Luke 23:34).

One of the most difficult things after praying is to wait upon God for the answer. It may take two weeks, two years, or, as in Abram's request for a son, 25 years for our prayers to be answered. This principle of waiting is revealed in the life of Abram and Sarai, who had no children. **Abram prayed for a son** and *said, Lord GOD, what will You give me, seeing I go* (remain) *childless? . . . You have given me no seed* (You have not answered my prayer for a son). *. . . And, behold, the word of the LORD came to him, saying . . . he that shall come forth out of your own bowels* (body) *shall be your heir* (Genesis 15:2-4).

Although God had promised Abram a son when he was 75 (see 12:4-7), he still had no son when he was 85 years old. At that time, *Sarai said to Abram . . . the LORD has restrained* (kept) *me from bearing . . . go in to my maid; it may be that I may obtain children* (build a family) *by her* (16:2). At the age of 86, Abram received a son, Ishmael, through Hagar (16:16).

Thirteen years passed after the birth of Ishmael.

Then God again spoke to Abram and changed his name: *I am the Almighty God. . . . Your name shall no more be called Abram, but your name shall be Abraham. . . . I will establish My Covenant* (Agreement) *between Me and you and. . . . with Isaac, which Sarah shall bear to you at this set time in the next year* (17:1-21). Abraham means *father of multitudes* (17:5).

By then, Abraham was 99 years old and Sarah was 90. At her age, it was humanly impossible for Sarah to have a child. But God revealed to Abraham: *I am the Almighty God,* meaning, the One who is All-Sufficient. God wants all of us to follow the example of Abraham, of whom God said: *I know him . . . he will command his children and his household after him, and they shall keep the way of the* LORD, *to do justice and judgment; that the* LORD *may bring upon Abraham that which He has spoken of him* (18:19).

Earlier God had said to Abram: *Walk before Me, and be . . . perfect* (blameless, devoted to God) (17:1). In our covenant relationship with the Lord, we have the same privilege of receiving answers to our prayers as Abraham had, and we have the same "responsibility of faith" as Abraham had.

God has chosen to develop our faith and bring about **His purposes on earth through our prayers.**

*If you abide in Me, and My words abide in you, **you shall ask what you will, and it shall be done to you*** (John 15:7). As we wait on God for answers to our prayers, we have His promise: *They that wait upon* (expectantly trust in) *the* LORD *shall renew their strength* (Isaiah 40:31).

We must learn to wait in the presence of God to obtain all that is promised! Surely this is one of the reasons that the Holy Spirit was led to remind us through the Apostle Paul: *Cast not away . . . your confidence, which has great recompence* (satisfaction) *of reward* (in heaven). *For you have need of patience* (endurance), *that, after you have done the will of God, you might receive the promise* (Hebrews 10:35-36).

Most men of God know something about waiting – Moses in the desert, David in the wilderness, Daniel in exile; and Paul in Arabia. The Prophet Micah proclaimed: *I will look to the* LORD: *I will wait for the God of my salvation: My God will hear me* (Micah 7:7).

When the death of a loved one occurs, it is difficult to wait through the long night of sorrow or bereavement. How easy it is to give way to anguish with extended days or months of tears and feelings of hopelessness, and to be angry at God! Yet, our

Father in heaven is the God of hope for a brighter tomorrow. We know that, regardless of our suffering, we can, **through prayer, commit our situation into the loving hands of our Father.** Therefore, we *sorrow not . . . . . . as others who have no hope* (I Thessalonians 4:13).

Thought for the day: *The LORD is good to them that wait for Him, to the soul that seeks Him* (Lamentations 3:25).

In Jesus' Name, Oh Lord, I pray
That Thou wilt guide me day by day
Keep my heart set on things Above
And fill me with Thy gracious love.

Do Thou my Stay and Comfort be
My Strength, my All — I trust in Thee —
Then shall communion be complete
My life and service for Thee — meet.

Live out Thy life, Oh Christ, each day
In this poor body made of clay,
Reveal again, through me, dear Lord
The mighty power of Thine own Word.

Jacob

*I*n contrast with Esau, *Jacob was a plain man, dwelling in tents* (Genesis 25:27). The Hebrew word for *plain* is the same word translated in other Scripture as *perfect, upright, undefiled;* so the word *plain* refers to Jacob's character as a man of God. God records His highest praise and blessing for Jacob: *The LORD has chosen Jacob to Himself* (Psalm 135:4).

Twenty years had passed since Jacob had built an altar **and prayed at Bethel** (see Genesis 28:18-22) on his way to his mother's kindred in Padan-aram, about 500 miles distance. During that time God had wonderfully blessed Jacob. But, the greed of Laban (Jacob's father-in-law) and his sons eventually resulted in a hostile attitude toward Jacob, the servant of God. Therefore, *the LORD said to Jacob, Return to the land of your fathers . . . and I will be with you. . . . I am the God of Bethel, where you . . . vowed a vow* **(prayed a promise)** *to Me: now arise, get . . . out from this land, and return to the land of your kindred* (31:3,13).

Jacob then began his long journey home with his two wives, two concubines, 11 sons and one daughter, and many servants and flocks. Jacob's brother Esau, who had threatened to kill Jacob (see 27:41-45), was approaching with 400 men, and Jacob was greatly afraid (see 32:3,6-7). **He earnestly prayed**: *O God of my father Abraham . . . the LORD who said to me, Return to your country, and to your kindred, and I will deal well with you. . . . And You said, I will surely do you good, and make your seed* (descendants) *as the sand of the sea, which cannot be numbered for multitude* (32:9-12).

The prayers of Jacob stand out as a bright star on a dark night. **His prayers lead us to see that we need to know the promises of God** as well as the conditions required to insure their fulfillment. We too need to remind the Lord that we are relying on His Word. **Most important, Jacob was praying for the future fulfillment of the covenant promise** that God had made to his grandfather Abraham (see 12:1-3). This promise was concerning the Messiah, the Lord Jesus Christ.

The Hebrew word *Yaacov* (Jacob) is translated "supplanter." One of the definitions of supplant in Webster's Dictionary is "to take the place of and serve as a substitute for, especially by reason of superior excellence."

This godly and humble servant of the Lord spent the **night alone, praying intensely**, until he was conferred with one of the highest honors given by God to any man in biblical history: *Your name shall be called no more Jacob, but Israel* (God prevails): *for as a prince you have power with God and with men, and have prevailed* (overcome) (32:28). Through the centuries, the people of God would be called by his name – Israel. Through his son Judah, Jesus the Messiah was promised (49:10; see Luke 3:23-34).

Some have been influenced by Esau's accusation condemning Jacob as a cheat. However, God had a different viewpoint and warned Christians to *follow (pursue) . . . holiness . . . lest any man fail of the grace of God . . . lest there be any fornicator, or profane* (godless) *person, as Esau, who for one morsel of meat sold his birthright. For . . . he was rejected* (Hebrews 12:14-17). *It is written, Jacob have I loved, but Esau have I hated* (detested) (Romans 9:13).

We too are in a covenant relationship with our Heavenly Father through Jesus Christ our Savior (see Matthew 26:28), who is our Mediator in prayers to God. *Thy kingdom come. Thy will be done* (6:10). *It is Christ . . . at the right hand of God, who also makes intercession for us* (Romans 8:34).

I asked the Lord that I might grow
In faith and love and every grace,
Might more of His salvation know
And seek more earnestly His face.

'Twas He who taught me thus to pray,
And He, I know, has answered prayer;
But it has been in such a way
As almost drove me to despair.

I thought that in some favored hour
At once, He'd answer my request,
And by His love's constraining power
Subdue my sins, and give me rest.

Instead of this, He made me feel
The hidden evils of my heart,
Let all the angry power of hell
Assault my soul in every part.

Nay, more, by His own hand He seemed
Intent to aggravate my woe,
Crossed all the fair designs I schemed,
Blasted my hopes, and laid me low.

"Lord, why is this?" I trembling cried,
"Wilt Thou pursue Thy worm to death?"
"'Tis in this way," the Lord replied,
"I answer prayer for grace and faith."

"These inward trials I employ
From sin and self to set thee free,
Blast all thy hopes of earthly joy
That thou mayest find thine all in Me."

Moses' Prayer for Miriam

 $\mathcal{M}$ iriam was the sister of Moses and of Aaron the high priest. She was honored above all the women of Israel, had a prophetic anointing, and was gifted in music and singing (Exodus 15:20; Micah 6:4).

However, *Miriam and Aaron spoke against Moses because of the Ethiopian* (Cushite) *woman whom he had married.... And they said, Has the* LORD *indeed spoken only by Moses? has He not spoken also by us? And the* LORD *heard it* (Numbers 12:1-2) – He always does. Since she no longer was as close to Moses as she had been, was she jealous that another woman had taken her place?

Suddenly, the Lord demanded to meet with Moses, Aaron, and Miriam. Miriam may have been delighted, assuming that God was just as displeased with Moses as she was and would agree with her criticism. Undoubtedly, she experienced an overwhelming shock when God said to them: *With him* (Moses) *I will speak mouth to mouth ... why then were you not afraid to speak against My servant Moses? And the anger of the* LORD *was kindled against them.... and, behold, Miriam became leprous, white as snow: and Aaron looked upon Miriam, and, behold, she was leprous. And Aaron said to Moses, Alas, my lord, I beseech you, lay not the sin upon us, wherein we have done foolishly, and wherein we have sinned* (12:8-11).

After Aaron's confession of their sin, **Moses prayed to the LORD, saying, Heal her now, O God, I pray** (12:13). It is more than coincidental that God declared that Moses was meek (humble), not weak (12:3). His prayer for his leprous sister brought about complete healing of that incurable disease.

When pride comes, then comes shame: but with the lowly is wisdom (Proverbs 11:2).

Covetousness and pride are very deceptive and are never satisfied. Even the possession of spiritual gifts is no safeguard against pride which, in turn, can lead to jealousy if others with similar spiritual gifts appear to be competitors. When someone whom we believe to be less qualified is promoted above us in our church or in our workplace and is given recognition, we may be tempted to fall into Miriam's sin of criticizing.

Pride takes many forms. It can be based on physical beauty, wealth, education, or talents; but pride is a self-destructive and self-deceptive sin that hinders our relationship with God and keeps our **prayers from being answered**. Covetous people never get enough money; proud people never get enough praise; and self-centered people never get enough attention. All three are hindrances to answered prayer. *Pride goes before destruction, and a haughty spirit before a fall* (16:18).

Miriam, as many others have, attempted to make it appear that her concern came from a "spiritual" motive. But God saw through her jealousy, envy, pride, and hurt feelings. It's human nature not to recognize certain things in our lives that must be forsaken if we are to have answers to our prayers.

When our lives are in harmony with God's Word, **our prayers will be answered**.

As we **kneel before God and pray**, we need the heartfelt concern of the psalmist of old who prayed: *Search me, O God, and know my heart: try me, and know my thoughts: And see if there be any wicked way in me* (Psalm 139:23-24).

Jesus assured His followers: *You are clean through the Word which I have spoken to you* (John 15:3). **In answer to our prayers**, our eyes are opened to *behold wondrous things out of God's Law* (the Word of God) (Psalm 119:18). As we read His Word, we receive wisdom (see James 1:5) to know God's will, and we receive strength to daily live in preparation for His return.

Receiving answers to prayer and studying the Bible go hand in hand. As we **meet with God in prayer** and read His Word (listen to what He is saying to us), *we continue to behold* (in the Word of God) *as in a mirror the glory of the Lord,* (and) *continue to be transfigured into His very own image in ever increasing splendor* (see II Corinthians 3:18).

Thought for the day: *The words of the* LORD *are pure words* (Psalm 12:6).

God's Holy Word has surely been
Inspired of God and not of men;
No power of eloquence of men
Could ever conceive God's wondrous plan.

Withstanding all the tests of time,
It stands unchanged, unique, sublime;
Proving to every tongue and race,
God's wisdom, mercy, love and grace.

So hammer on, ye hostile hands;
Your hammers break, God's anvil stands.

Moses' Prayer for Israel

Leaving the wilderness of Sinai, the Lord led the Israelites northward until they reached Kadesh-barnea – just 11 days' journey from Mount Sinai. The march from Egypt, including the 12-month stay at Mount Sinai (Horeb), had taken about 16 months. Now they stood on the threshold of Canaan – the glorious land that God had promised to give them. A leader from each of the twelve tribes had taken 40 days to spy out the land. When they returned, carrying a single cluster of grapes so large it took two men to carry it, the Israelites were assured of the extraordinary fruitfulness of Canaan (see Numbers 13:23,27).

However, ten of the spies discouraged the people, saying: *The people are strong that dwell in the land, and the cities are walled, and very great* (13:28). But Caleb, one of the 12, was quick to say: *Let us go up at once, and possess it; for we are well able to overcome it* (13:30). Nevertheless, *all the congregation lifted up their voice* (made loud lament), *and cried; and the people wept that night. And all the children of*

Israel murmured (grumbled against God) . . . *would God* (we wish) *we had died in this wilderness!* (14:1-2).

The people concluded: *Let us make a captain, and let us return into Egypt. . . . the LORD said to Moses. . . . I will smite* (strike) *them . . . and disinherit them, and will make of you a greater nation and mightier than they* (14:4-12).

If Moses' ambition had been to make himself great, this would have been his opportunity; but, he never responded to the great honor and opportunity that God had offered him. Instead, he prayed: *The LORD is long-suffering, and of great mercy, forgiving iniquity. . . . Pardon, I beseech You, the iniquity of this people according to the greatness of Your mercy, and as You have forgiven this people, from Egypt even until now. And the LORD said, I have pardoned according to your word* (14:18-20).

This is one of the most exemplary and admirable prayers in the Bible. Moses' deepest desire was to honor God, honor God's Word, honor God's faithfulness, and honor *the greatness of God's mercy.* He was pleading the honor of God's Name among the heathen, and **his prayer was answered immediately.**

However, the Israelites' rebellion brought about

the end of their journey to the land of promise and the beginning of 38 years of wilderness wanderings during which all who were 20 years and older, except for Caleb and Joshua, *died in this wilderness* as they had rashly said (14:2).

The effectiveness of Moses' prayer was the result of his desire to magnify the Lord – not himself. This ought to be an encouragement to each one of us to **pray when the answer would seem impossible**. Yes, God is *the same yesterday, and to day, and for ever* (Hebrews 13:8).

Answers to our prayers and the blessings of God upon our lives are dependent upon our faith in the promises of God, regardless of how impossible the circumstances appear, like Abraham who *believed . . . God . . . and calls those things which be not as though they were* (Romans 4:17). This incident should also serve as a warning of how complaining and depression destroy a person's faith and spiritual progress. The choice is entirely up to us. We can decide to be like Caleb and Joshua, who believed that God would keep His promises; or we can decide to be like the majority of the Israelites – dissatisfied and depressed over unexpected circumstances. Faith in the prayer promises of God is evidenced by an attitude of *rejoice in the Lord always: and again I say, Rejoice* (Philippians 4:4), and *in every thing give thanks: for this is the will of God in Christ Jesus concerning you* (I Thessalonians 5:18). But, **answers to our prayers also depend upon our desire that the answer to our prayers will glorify the Lord**.

After nearly 40 years, the second generation of Israelites finally was near its last encampment and would soon cross the Jordan River to enter the promised land. Some of them were children when their parents left Egypt, while others had been born in the wilderness. Regrettably, their attitude was similar to that of their parents (see Numbers 21:4-5). Because of finding fault with God's arrangement of their circumstances, *the LORD sent fiery serpents . . . and many people of Israel died* (21:6).

When they repented, *Moses prayed for them,* and God's response to Moses' *prayer* was immediate. *The LORD said to Moses, Make . . . a fiery serpent* (of brass), *and set it upon a pole: and it shall come to pass, that every one that is bitten, when he looks upon it, shall live* (21:7-8). The brass serpent was a symbol of God's judgment for their sin and of His mercy and love for all who repented and truly believed in Him. The salvation of those who followed God's orders to look upon the serpent of brass confirms **the power of just one person's intercessory prayer**. God desires to answer our prayers even more than we desire answers. We also need to understand that *these things happened to them for examples: and they are written for our admonition* (serious reminder) (I Corinthians 10:11).

Moses, Joshua, and Caleb stood alone against the majority opinion of an estimated two million people. **Miraculous answers to prayer are not the result of a majority but the faith of a believing minority**.

Many centuries later, in His conversation with *Nicodemus, a ruler of the Jews* (John 3:1-21), Jesus said that the *serpent* which had been lifted up by Moses in the wilderness illustrated Himself as the One to *be lifted up* on the cross as the only way for sinners to be saved from eternal death (see 3:14-15; 12:32). Jesus did not tell Nicodemus how he should live to have eternal life; rather, He told him how to be made alive and brought into a right relationship with God. Jesus replied to Nicodemus: *Verily, verily, I say to you, Except a man be born of water and of the Spirit, he cannot enter into the Kingdom of God* (3:5). This is far more than giving up bad habits or turning over a new leaf.

All mankind, with one exception (Jesus, the sinless Son of God), was *dead in trespasses and sins* (Ephesians 2:1). Each of us was born with our parents' sinful human nature, but Jesus was born of the Virgin Mary by an act of God (Luke 1:35) so Jesus was without sin. A person's first prayer should be for salvation: *God be merciful to me a sinner* (18:13). After we receive Christ as our Savior, we then are qualified to pray to "Our Father."

Thought for the day: *He shall call upon Me, and I will answer him: I will be with him in trouble; I will deliver him, and honor him* (Psalm 91:15).

We hide in our Refuge,
Christ Jesus the Lord
And know Thou wilt keep us
through Thy Holy Word;
In Thee we have shelter,
and no other place —
Thou alone canst afford us
Thy bountiful grace.

When Joshua Failed to Pray

*A*fter 40 years of wandering in the wilderness, the long-awaited moment had arrived. The Lord held back the waters of the Jordan River at the time of year when it normally overflowed its banks, *and all the Israelites passed over on dry ground* into Canaan (Joshua 3:6-17).

More than six times in the first six chapters of the Book of Joshua we read that the Lord had directed Joshua and that whatever the Lord said, Joshua did (1:1-9; 3:7-8; 4:1-3,8,10,15-16; 5:2,15; 6:2,5; 11:15). *And Joshua said to the children of Israel . . . hear the words of the LORD your God. And . . . you shall know* (understand) *that the living God is among you. . . . your God dried up the waters of the Jordan . . . that all the people of the earth might know the hand of the LORD, that it is mighty: that you might fear* (reverence) *the LORD your God for ever. . . . And the Captain of the LORD's host said to Joshua. . . . I have given into your hand Jericho* (3:9-10; 4:23-24; 5:15; 6:2).

The Israelites' victory over Jericho was amazing as the fortified walls of the city fell inward.

They rejoiced over the miraculous victory; however, without **praying for further direction** from God, they attacked the city of Ai. *The men of Ai smote of them about thirty and six men: for they chased them . . . and smote them in the going down* (the descent or slope) (7:5).

Joshua had failed to pray and seek the will of God. The Lord Himself was their Commander-in-Chief, and He alone could provide victory in their conquest of Canaan (see 1:5). Joshua learned how easy it is to be deceived when relying on the advice of mere *men* (7:2) as to how to conquer the *few men of Ai* (7:3-4). **By not consulting the Lord in prayer,** Israel's defeat was inevitable (see 7:5). After the shocking defeat and death of 36 Israelite soldiers, Joshua at first blamed God and prayed: *Alas, O Lord GOD, wherefore have You . . . brought this people over Jordan. . . . the Canaanites . . . shall hear of it . . . and what will you do to Your great Name?* (7:7-9).

All of us are prone to blame God or question His concern when things do not happen as we anticipated. First, the evil sin of Achan had to be judged (see 7:10-26). Then, when Joshua called on the Lord, He directed him in the complete victory over Ai.

The Israelites' reasoning that led to their defeat

at Ai has been repeated by most of us. When no serious problems seem to exist, we become over-confident and self-sufficient, and assume the Lord expects us to use "our own good judgment." However, apart from our **submission to the indwelling presence of the Holy Spirit and daily prayer for guidance**, the smallest temptation may prove to be too powerful for us. He alone imparts discernment when we seek His will as revealed in His Word.

When everything is going our way, it is easy to forget that **God has a definite plan for our future endeavors**. It is foolish to assume that just because He guided us a certain way in one situation, He will guide the same way the next time. That's why it is so **important that we pray for guidance in making each decision**.

Many begin their Christian lives in prayer and daily Bible reading, but then gradually become self-confident and forget that *God resists the proud, and gives grace to the humble. Humble yourselves therefore under the mighty hand of God, that He may exalt you in due time* (I Peter 5:5-6). The truth is that we don't win our victories just because we are Christians anymore than Joshua won the battle at Ai simply because he was an Israelite. The purposes of God in our lives are only fulfilled when we are in submission to His will.

After Joshua's victories over Jericho and Ai, the forces of Satan became more intense. Five kings united to fight the Israelites and, then, the unsuspected happened as it often does when we become **overconfident and fail to pray**. The Gibeonites, who lived between the land of the Canaanite kings and the encampment of Israel (see Joshua 9:17), decided their chances of survival would be greater by making a league with the Israelites than by joining with the Canaanite kings in their war against Israel.

Under false pretenses, their delegation approached Joshua and said: *From a very far country your servants are come because of the Name* (reputation) *of the* LORD *your God: for we have heard the fame of Him, and all that He did in Egypt.... Wherefore our elders and all the inhabitants of our country spoke to us, saying, Take victuals* (provisions, food) *with you for the journey, and go to meet them, and say to them, We are your servants: therefore now make you a league* (treaty) *with us.... And the men ... **asked not counsel ... of the* LORD **(did not pray)**. *And Joshua made peace with them, and made a league with them, to let them live* (9:9,11,14-15). Although it was a compromise, it seemed like a peaceful solution to accept the Gibeonites' suggestion. However, in doing so, they were in violation of the Law of God (see Exodus 23:31-33; 34:12). The moldy bread and worn clothing seemed to be visible proof of the strangers' words (Joshua 9:12-13). Too often we foolishly make decisions based on what we see or think. But being ignorant of God's Word does not nullify the results of not seeking His guidance.

This league with the Gibeonites should impress upon us the enemy's skill in deception. We should also recognize how fallible our human reasoning is. **If Joshua had prayed for the Lord's guidance**, God would have exposed the Gibeonites' deception, and the league never would have been made.

The Israelites honored the oath they had sworn to the Gibeonites *by the Lord God of Israel* (9:18) even though the Gibeonites had deceived them. However, over 400 years later, King Saul broke this covenant, and it resulted in a 3-year famine in Israel (II Samuel 21:1). Through this, the Lord reveals that the wrong done by another does not give us the right to do a similar wrong. One sin never justifies another. We also learn **how important it is to pray** for the Lord to *lead us not into temptation, but* *deliver us from evil* (Matthew 6:13).

A characteristic of the children of God that distinguishes us from all other people is that we *overcome evil with good* (Romans 12:21). From Joshua's mistake in making a covenant with the Gibeonites God wants us to learn how important it is to pray for guidance before we make decisions. Our spiritual victories depend on whether or not we do God's will. It is also important to have personal integrity and keep our commitments, even when they may be unpleasant. Once again we are reminded: *Trust in the LORD with all your heart; and lean not to your own understanding. In all your ways acknowledge Him, and He shall direct your paths* (Proverbs 3:5-6).

Thought for the day: *It is a good thing to give thanks to the LORD, and to sing praises to Your Name, O Most High: To show forth Your lovingkindness in the morning, and Your faithfulness every night* (Psalm 92:1-2).

Gideon

*A*t one time during the 450-year period of the Judges (see Acts 13:20), the Israelites were enslaved by the Midianites. The reason was obvious: *The children of Israel did evil* (sinned) *in the sight of the LORD: And the LORD delivered them into the hand* (under the control) *of Midian seven years. . . . And Israel was greatly impoverished* (Judges 6:1,6). **Eventually the Israelites *cried* (prayed) *to the LORD* (6:6). The answer to their prayers was not what they expected.** It began with reproof: *The LORD sent a prophet . . . which said to them, Thus says the LORD God of Israel, I brought you up from Egypt . . . out of the hand of all that oppressed you, and drove them out from before you, and gave you their land . . . but you have not obeyed My voice* (6:8-10). There was no word of comfort or assurance of relief from their suffering – only reproof. The people were left with the consciousness of how sinful they had been. They needed to recognize that their miserable circumstances were the direct result of their willful disregard for the Word of God.

It would appear that this unnamed prophet

may have had only one convert – Gideon: *The Angel of the Lord appeared to him, and said . . . The Lord is with you, you mighty man of valor. . . . Go in this your might, and you shall save Israel from the hand of the Midianites* (6:12,14).

Gideon was deeply conscious of his poverty, his lack of resources, and his own lack of ability, **but he prayed:** *Oh my Lord, wherewith shall I save Israel? behold, my family is poor in Manasseh, and I am the least in my father's house* (6:15).

Some people tend to think God cannot use them because, like Moses, they are not a fluent speaker (see Exodus 4:10-16); or, they are like Gideon who was *poor . . . and the least in his father's house.* Some have the misconceived idea that the only people God can use are those who are educated, wealthy, have superior talents, or have influence in their communities. But, often these people are too busy, want to do things their way, or would rather compromise than lose their popularity. In fact, many of them don't even belong to the Lord because they have never trusted Christ as Savior. Faith in God, not in our wisdom or ability, is the foundation for being used of God.

Gideon was truly a man of inexperience and

uncertainty, but he obeyed the Lord. Gideon was ready to worship the God of Israel, and he *built an altar there to the* LORD, *and called it Jehovah-Shalom* (the Lord is peace) (6:24).

The Lord could count on the loyalty of Gideon. Can He count on us? Like Gideon, we must not allow fear or circumstances to govern our decisions; rather, we must remain faithful to Jesus, who said: *If you love Me, keep My commandments* (John 14:15). And then He added: *If you abide* (live) *in Me, and My words abide in you,* **you shall ask (pray)** *what you will, and it shall be done to you. . . . Verily* (Truly), *verily, I say to you,* **Whatsoever you shall ask (pray for)** *the Father in My Name, He will give it to you. . . . ask in My Name: and . . . I will pray the Father for you* (on your behalf): *For the Father Himself loves you, because you have loved Me* (15:7; 16:23,26-27).

Thought for the day: *Whatsoever you do in word or deed, do all in the Name of the Lord Jesus, giving thanks to God and the Father by Him* (Colossians 3:17).

Jephthah

*A*fter 18 years of suffering oppression (see Judges 10:8) as a result of God's judgment, *the children of Israel said* **(prayed)** *to the* L<small>ORD</small>, *We have sinned....* *And they put away the strange gods* (foreign idols) *from among them, and served the* L<small>ORD</small> (10:15-16). When *the Ammonites made war against Israel, the elders of Gilead went to bring Jephthah out of the land of Tob* (a district in Syria): *And they said... Come, and be our captain, that we may fight with the Ammonites* (11:5-6).

Before going to war, **Jephthah prayed:** *If You shall without fail deliver the children of Ammon into my hands, Then it shall be, that whatever comes forth of the doors of my house to meet me, when I return* in peace... *shall surely be the* L<small>ORD</small>*'s, and I will offer it up for a burned offering* (11:30-31). Jephthah left the outcome as to what his sacrifice would be in the Lord's hands. **God answered his prayer and gave him victory** over the Ammonites. In that time and culture, homes were built so that the animals could live on the ground level beneath the family dwelling. Jephthah probably expected a sheep or some other animal to come out the door.

But, everything that happened next was of God who, in His providence, arranged that Jephthah's daughter should be the first to come out this ground level door to meet him. It was as if God were saying: "I have given you all you asked – your restoration, your leadership, and the freedom of Israel from oppression; now I ask you to give Me your only child in return." Jephthah had promised in prayer: *Whatever . . . shall surely be the LORD's* (11:31).

This could not have meant he offered his daughter as a human sacrifice, as some have supposed. Jephthah knew the Scriptures well, as expressed in his messages to the Ammonites (11:12-27). God had condemned human sacrifices as an abominable and evil practice of heathen worship (Leviticus 20:2-5; Deuteronomy 12:29-31; 18:10-12). How could it be imagined that Jephthah would cut the throat of his daughter to offer her as a burned offering upon an altar and believe that *she shall surely be the LORD's*! To do that would have made God, as well as this man of faith, responsible for a vile murder. It was *the Spirit of the LORD* who had given Jephthah his victory (Judges 11:29,32). Obviously we must interpret Jephthah's statement: *I will offer it up for a burned offering* (11:31) to mean something acceptable under the Law.

How Jephthah fulfilled his vow becomes clear as we consider all the facts. First: *She was his only child; beside her he had neither son nor daughter* (11:34). The Lord had declared that the firstborn were to be "sanctified" – not sacrificed: *The firstborn are Mine* (Exodus 13:2; Numbers 3:13). And Jephthah's daughter's response to his vow made the outcome unmistakably clear. She asked for *two months* to go up and down the mountains of Israel to *bewail her virginity* (Judges 11:37) – meaning to "bewail the fact that she would never marry" – not to "bewail her death on an altar." Undoubtedly, in lifelong chastity, she became one of the servants of God in the Tabernacle at Shiloh. And, to remove all possible doubt, we read that Jephthah *did with her according to his vow which he had vowed: and she knew no man* (she never married) (11:39). She was dedicated to serve the Lord, even as Hannah dedicated Samuel as a "spiritual" burned offering to the Lord.

Like Abraham before him, Jephthah's love for, and trust in, God was tested: and, like Abraham, he passed the test and also was highly honored by the Lord as one of the heroes of the faith as recorded in the inspired Word of God: **Jephthah** ... **David** *also, and* **Samuel**, *and* ... *the prophets: Who through faith subdued kingdoms,* **wrought** **(served the cause of)** **righteousness** (Hebrews 11:32-33). The heroes of faith were ordinary men and women like Jephthah, and like Abraham, who *believed God, and it was counted to him for righteousness* (Romans 4:3). They all are examples to us of how God will sovereignly move in the lives of those who submit to His will and trust in Him. From them we learn that *faith is the substance* (assurance) *of things hoped for, the evidence* (conviction) *of things not seen* (Hebrews 11:1).

Above all, taking the shield of faith, wherewith you shall be able to quench (put out) *all the fiery darts* (arrows, shots) *of the wicked. And take the helmet of salvation, and the Sword of the Spirit, which is the Word of God:* **Praying always with all prayer and supplication in the Spirit**, *and watching thereto with all perseverance and* **supplication for all saints** (Ephesians 6:16-18).

In the early church, as recorded in the Book of Acts, with the multiplied responsibilities that had come upon the apostles, *the twelve called the multitude of the disciples to them, and said.* ... *we will give ourselves* **continually to prayer, and to the ministry**

48

of the Word (Acts 6:2-4). With the apostles as our example, we realize that prayer is the means that God has provided for our receiving mercy and obtaining grace *to help in the time of need* (Hebrews 4:16).

Prayer in the Name of Jesus results in fullness of joy. Jesus confirmed this truth when He said: *Until now have you asked nothing in My Name: ask, and you shall receive, that your joy may be full* (John 16:24).

One of the sobering warnings of God concerning the necessity to pray is: *Take heed to yourselves, lest at any time your hearts be overcharged* (overpowered) *with surfeiting* (self-indulgence), *and drunkenness, and cares* (pleasures) *of this life . . . so that day* (of Christ's return) *come upon you unawares* (suddenly). *For as a snare it shall come on all them that dwell on the face of the whole earth. Watch . . . therefore, and pray always, that you may be accounted worthy to escape all these things that shall come to pass, and to stand before the Son of Man* (Luke 21:34-36).

Reading His Word and praying with a sincere desire to please the Lord can root out heresy, smooth out misunderstandings, sweep away jealousies and animosities, obliterate immoralities, and release the power to accomplish the will of God in our lives.

If we ignore the Word, we hinder *the Spirit* to

help *our infirmities*, for we have ignored the spiritual insight and strength God has provided in His Word to help us **understand how to pray effectively**.

Thought for the day: *Call upon Me, and I will answer him: I will be with him in trouble; I will deliver him, and honor him* (Psalm 91:15).

Not what I do, Lord, nor what I say,
But what I am, Lord, matters today.
Busy with nothing we fill up the years,
Hurrying, worrying, gathering tears.

Why can't I learn, Lord, that power is within,
Why can't I see, Lord, the waste of my sin?
If I could be, Lord, growing in soul,
Seeing each day, Lord, more clearly the goal.

If I could live, Lord, discerning thy face,
Ever more strongly held by thy grace;
So take and mold, Lord this heart of mine,
Till it shall be, Lord, like unto thine!

Hannah's Silent Prayer

*N*ear the end of the period of the Judges, a few great men and women of faith prayed and received remarkable answers to their prayers. Among them was Hannah, a godly woman who was married to a man who had two wives. Having multiple wives was customary then as a means of continuing a family heritage when the first wife couldn't have children. Because Hannah could not have children, she had lived many years in deep sorrow and humiliation, for the Hebrew culture considered barrenness a disgrace. However, Hannah remained a faithful worshiper of God and, *year by year, when she went up to the house of the* LORD *. . . the other wife provoked her . . . she* (Hannah) *wept, and did not eat. . . .* In desperation **she vowed a vow** (prayed), *and said, O* LORD *of hosts, if You will indeed look on the affliction of Your handmaid, and remember me, and . . . give to Your handmaid a man* (male) *child, then I will give him to the* LORD *all the days of his life* (I Samuel 1:7,11). *And it came to pass, as* **she continued praying** *before the* LORD, *that Eli* (the priest) *marked* (noticed) *her mouth. Now Hannah . . . spoke in her heart; only her lips moved . . . therefore Eli thought she was drunk. And Eli said to her, How long will you be drunken?* (1:12-14). Although she was wrongfully accused, Hannah did not become angry; instead, she graciously answered Eli: *No, my lord, I am a woman of a sorrowful spirit: I have drunk neither wine nor strong drink, but have poured out my soul before the Lord* (1:15-16).

As high priest, it was Eli's responsibility to rebuke those who did evil. In this case, Eli's misjudgment was truly a test of the genuineness of Hannah's humility. Had she reacted in indignation and anger toward Eli for being so judgmental, she would have returned home with a bitter attitude. However, instead of being angry, she appealed to Eli by telling him of her sorrow. *Then Eli answered and said, Go in peace: and the God of Israel grant you your petition that you have asked of Him* (1:17). For her humility and steadfast faith, the Lord granted her request for a son – then blessed her even more than she had requested. Each year, *the Lord visited Hannah, so that she* (eventually) *bore three sons and two daughters* (2:21). Her first son, the one **she had prayed for so fervently,** was Samuel, who also became **a great man of prayer** and, as Israel's last judge, united the tribes into one nation.

Although Hannah was a faithful worshiper of God, she lived centuries before the New Testament experience of being filled with the Holy Spirit or of having the privilege of reading what Paul wrote to the Ephesian Christians: *Praying always with all prayer and supplication in the Spirit, and watching thereto with all perseverance* (Ephesians 6:18).

Hannah knew very little of the Scriptures that we have today. However, when she was falsely accused by the priest of being drunk, Hannah maintained a godly attitude. **The acceptance of an undeserved rebuke in a right spirit often brings an answer to our prayers.**

Hannah had learned to pray and trust the Lord long before David wrote: *Delight yourself also in the* L*ORD; and He shall give you the desires of your heart. Commit your way to the* L*ORD; trust also in Him; and He shall bring it to pass* (Psalm 37:4-5).

Even though we read that *our Father knows what things we have need of, before we ask Him* (Matthew 6:8), in order to receive those *things*, our Father in heaven has given us the responsibility to release them by praying in the Name of Jesus. We are to **pray only to *our Father*** . . . *who gives good things* (what is good for us) *to them that ask Him* (7:11).

Only our Creator can fully know what is best for us. The God of perfect wisdom says of His children: *O that there were such a heart in them, that they would fear* (reverence) *Me, and keep* (obey) *all My Commandments always, that it might be well with them, and with their children for ever!* (Deuteronomy 5:29).

Thought for the Day: *Evening, and morning, and at noon, will I pray, and cry aloud: and He shall hear my voice* (Psalm 55:17).

Art thou abiding in the Vine
In fellowship serene,
His Precious Word, thy daily Bread
With naught thy Lord between?

My child, If thou wouldst ever abound
In Jesus Christ, thy Lord
Then truly thou must ever abide
In God's own Holy Word.

So, as we wait our Coming King
May we in Truth be found,
Clothed in His righteousness alone,
Abide — and thus Abound.

Samuel Prays

After Samuel became the judge of Israel, the Philistines were so badly defeated **because of his prayer meeting** at Mizpeh that *they came no more into the coast* (territory) *of Israel: and the hand of the LORD was against the Philistines all the days of Samuel* (I Samuel 7:13). However, *there was severe war against the Philistines all the days of Saul* (14:52). What made the difference? God wants us to know the far-reaching effect of **just one prayer** from someone that lived to please the Lord.

Samuel had faithfully led God's people; but eventually, they demanded a king to rule over them. God directed Samuel to anoint Saul to be Israel's first king.

In the first year of Saul's reign, in a spectacular defeat of the Ammonites, he proudly proclaimed to the people: *The LORD has wrought salvation in Israel* (11:13). But, King Saul soon ignored the Prophet Samuel who remained faithful to the Lord. We should remind ourselves of what Samuel the prophet said: *God forbid that I should sin against the*

LORD *in ceasing to pray for you* (12:23). But, Samuel did more than pray. He taught the people the necessity of obedience to God: *I will teach you the good and right way.*

Eventually, Saul chose his own way instead of God's way. In his fortieth year as king, the Philistines gathered soldiers together and prepared for war against the Israelites. Saul panicked when he was told the size of the Philistine armies that were ready to attack, and **he prayed**. This is the only record of Saul praying for guidance during his 40-year reign. But *the LORD did not answer him* (28:6).

How could Saul have forgotten that the Prophet Samuel had declared: *Because you have rejected the Word of the LORD, He has also rejected you* (15:23)? Saul had attempted to murder David many times and had forced him into exile. Blinded by jealousy and his hatred of David, Saul accused Ahimelech, the high priest, of conspiring to protect David and ordered the execution of Ahimelech and all the priests and their families. Without hesitation, when Saul gave the command, *Doeg the Edomite . . . slew on that day fourscore and five* (85) *persons . . . men and women, children* (22:18-20).

How pathetic it is to see Saul – who at the

beginning of his reign was mightily blessed of God – riding through the night, frantically seeking advice from a fortune-teller in Endor! He knew that mediums, spiritualists, witches, and fortune-tellers *are an abomination to the* LORD (Deuteronomy 18:10-12). In fact, in the early years of Saul's reign he had banished these evil people from the land (I Samuel 28:3). The woman that had *a familiar spirit at Endor* (28:7,9), like all fortune-tellers, was no help. Instead, Saul's fears increased even more after the appearance of the deceased Prophet Samuel, who said: *Why . . . do you ask of me, seeing the* LORD *is departed from you, and is become your enemy?* (28:16).

The next day Saul, along with three of his sons, including Jonathan, was killed in battle (see 31:1-6). Finally, Saul reaped what he had sown. When man rejects the light of God's Word, he leaves himself open to spiritual deception the way Saul did. Saul's worst enemy was not the Philistines, but himself. He had lived a self-serving life.

Power, pride, wealth, popularity, and talents are all wonderful gifts from God, but they can become great hindrances if we fail to use them to honor God. Often these gifts can cause people to reject *the Word of the* LORD, as Saul did. Some today still seek guidance from psychics, fortune-tellers, and palm readers rather than **praying to the Lord** in times of great distress and relying upon Him.

We also need to remind ourselves of David's prayer: *For You, Lord, are good, and ready to forgive; and plenteous in mercy to all them that call upon You.* **Give ear, O Lord, to my prayer; and attend to the voice of my supplications (prayers). In the day of my trouble I will call upon You: for You will answer me** (Psalm 86:5-7).

Thought for the day: *The Lord knows the way of the righteous: but the way of the ungodly shall perish* (Psalm 1:6).

Only a smile, yes, only a smile
That a woman over-burdened with grief
Expected from you,
'twoud have given her relief
For her heart ached sore the while.
But weary and cheerless she went her way
Because, as it happened, that very day
You were out of touch with your Lord.

David's Prayer
When Absalom Led a Revolt

After Absalom had his older half-brother Amnon murdered for raping Absalom's sister, he remained in exile three years with his grandfather, his mother's father, who was king of Geshur (Syria) (see II Samuel 13:28-38). After about three years, Joab, commander-in-chief of David's army, initiated a deceptive plan to persuade David to allow Absalom to return home without being executed for his crime.

Two years later, after Absalom returned to Israel (14:28) with a defiant attitude, he demanded that Joab arrange to have the king see him. David promptly forgave Absalom, who then began an ambitious and wicked conspiracy to overthrow his father and declare himself king of Israel. *Absalom prepared . . . chariots and horses, and fifty men to run before him. And Absalom rose up early* (daily), *and stood beside the way* (entrance) *of the city gate* (where business affairs were often conducted)*: and . . . when any man that had a controversy* (lawsuit) *came to* *the king* (court) *for judgment* (to decide), *then Absalom* (pretended a deep concern and) *called to him, and said. . . . your matters are good and right; but there is no man deputed of* (representing) *the king to hear you. . . . Oh that I were made judge in the land, that every man which has any suit or cause might come to me, and I would do him justice!* (15:1-4). Soon the shocking news reached David that *the hearts of the men of Israel are after* (with) *Absalom* (15:13).

It is sad to read that there came a day when David, the brokenhearted old king, said to his servants: *Arise, and let us flee; or we will not . . . escape from Absalom: make speed to depart, lest he overtake us suddenly, and bring evil upon us, and smite the city with the edge of the sword* (15:14). David left Jerusalem, running barefoot down the rocky, rugged hill to the Brook Kidron and *up by the ascent of Mount Olivet, and wept as he went up,* fleeing Jerusalem in fear of Absalom, his own beloved son (15:30). But David expressed no words of self-pity, bitterness, or revenge. His greatest concern was to avoid bloodshed in the city of God.

It often takes a crisis to reveal who our true friends are as well as to **discover the wonderful way God has of answering our prayers**.

Even Ahithophel, David's most trusted advisor, accepted Absalom's invitation to join the conspiracy. Ahithophel became a traitor and, with Absalom, made plans to kill David.

The conspiracy was strong; for the people increased (in numbers) *continually with Absalom* (15:12). David appeared to be a helpless fugitive. He was old, and it appeared that Absalom had successfully won the confidence of most of the key leaders of the nation. When Ahithophel decided to desert David and join with Absalom, he revealed his true character with the words "me" and "I" being prominent as he spoke to Absalom: *Let me now choose out twelve thousand men, and I will arise and pursue after David this night: And I will come upon him . . . I will smite* (murder) *the king only: And I will bring back all the people to you* (17:1-3). At first, *the saying pleased Absalom* (17:4). But **God did not forget David's prayer**: *O LORD . . . turn the counsel of Ahithophel into foolishness* (15:31).

When Absalom rejected Ahithophel's advice on how to win the war, Ahithophel committed suicide. This powerful conspiracy was recorded in the Bible to strengthen our faith that **God can and will answer prayer when our situation appears hope-**

less by human calculations.

Pity those who are unaware of the "Unseen Presence" of God and **the power of prayer** when there is no place else to go. Without exception, **the Lord defends all who pray** and who live to please Him. *All things are naked and opened to the eyes of Him with whom we have to do. Seeing then that we have a great High Priest, that is passed into the heavens, Jesus the Son of God. . . . Let us therefore come boldly to the throne of grace, that we may obtain mercy, and find grace to help in time of need* (Hebrews 4:13-14,16). *For promotion comes neither from the east, nor from the west, nor from the south. But God is the judge: He puts down one, and sets up another* (Psalm 75:6-7).

Thought for the day: *The LORD is good, a stronghold (refuge) in the day of trouble; and He knows them that trust in Him* (Nahum 1:7).

*Day by day the manna fell —
Oh, to learn this lesson well:
Still by constant mercy fed,
Give us, Lord, our daily bread.*

The Prayer of Solomon

The day had arrived for the dedication of the glorious Temple in Jerusalem. *Then Solomon assembled the elders of Israel . . . in Jerusalem, that they might bring up the Ark of the Covenant of the LORD out of the city of David, which is Zion. . . . and the priests brought in the Ark of the Covenant of the LORD . . . into . . . the Most Holy Place* (I Kings 8:1,6).

The Israelites all stood in the courtyard, and Solomon *stood before the altar of the LORD . . . and spread forth his hands: For Solomon had made a brazen scaffold . . . and kneeled down upon his knees before all the congregation of Israel, and spread forth his hands toward heaven* (II Chronicles 6:12-13). It was not uncommon for the people of God to **lift their hands in prayer and praise** (see Psalm 63:3-4). Hands lifted toward heaven are a sign of wholehearted submission and worship. It should be natural to lift up our hands or to kneel in humility before the living Triune God.

Solomon prayed *that all people of the earth may know Your Name, to fear You, as do Your people Israel.*

Then *he . . . blessed . . . Israel . . . saying. . . . The LORD our God be with us . . . That He may incline* (turn) *our hearts to Him, to walk in all His ways, and to keep His Commandments. . . . That all the people of the earth may know that* **the LORD *is God***, *and that there is none else* (I Kings 8:43,55,57-58,60). This was a confirmation that Buddha, Allah, and all other "gods" are false gods and cannot answer prayer.

In Hebrew *Elohim*, one of the words most frequently translated as "God" in the Old Testament, is plural in form in keeping with the fact that the One True God is three Persons in One: God the Father; Jesus, who is God the Son; and God the Holy Spirit. A Christian's daily conversation and conduct should express adoration and loyalty to the One True God: *For there is one God, and one Mediator between God and men, the Man Christ Jesus* (I Timothy 2:5-6).

Sadly, **Solomon's conduct later in life didn't match his prayer of dedication**. It is pathetic to know there is no record that Solomon ever **prayed** any other prayers or repented of any of his many *outlandish* sins (see Nehemiah 13:26). Eventually we read: *The LORD was angry with Solomon, because his heart was turned from the LORD God of Israel, which had appeared to him twice* (I Kings 11:9).

After the great prayer of dedication with its petition for God to **hear Israel's prayers**, the Lord again
appeared to Solomon by night, saying: *If I shut up
heaven that there be no rain, or if I command the locusts
to devour the land, or if I send pestilence among My
people; If My people, which are called by My Name, shall
humble themselves, and pray, and seek My face*, and
*turn from their wicked ways; then I will hear from
heaven, and will forgive their sin, and will heal their
land* (II Chronicles 7:13-14; see also I Kings 3:5-15).

Carefully consider the qualifications for God to
heal their land. First, He is speaking to *My people*.
Today, *My people* are those who have received Christ
as personal Savior. Then, to *humble* ourselves and
turn from our wicked ways includes acknowledging
our sins, being sorry for our sins, and repenting of
(turning from) our sins. God alone can, and does,
forgive and cleanse us from all confessed sin. But,
God has warned: *He that turns away his ear from
hearing the Law, even his prayer shall be abomination*
(Proverbs 28:9).

When God says: *Seek My face*, He means for us to
daily seek His will by **reading His Word and praying**.

God has provided a way to teach everyone how
to cope with the problems all of us face. But He has

provided prayer as a means of bringing His will to pass. *The righteous cry, and the LORD hears, and delivers them out of all their troubles* (Psalm 34:17).

Thought for the day: *I will praise You, O Lord my God, with all my heart: and I will glorify Your Name for evermore* (Psalm 86:12).

Oh! Christ of God, live out Thy life
In this poor house of clay:
Keep Thou my spirit free from strife —
Resting in Thee each day.

Thou only art my Portion, Lord
— Boundless in grace and power —
The Light of Thine Eternal Word
Doth meet my need each hour.

The joy of God is ever my strength —
Fill constantly with joy,
Until, throughout its breadth and length,
My being Thou employ.

Such faith alone ever pleases Thee
— No less wilt Thou receive —
For time and for Eternity
Thou dost command, "Believe."

Hezekiah

*W*hen *Hezekiah* became king of Judah, he did not follow the ways of his evil father, Ahaz (II Kings 18:1). Instead, he believed the prophets of God *and did what was right in the sight of the LORD, according to all that David his father* (ancestor) *did* (18:3). We learn from Hezekiah that **people will be blessed and prayers will be answered when the Word of God is obeyed.**

Hezekiah was one of the most godly and greatest kings in the 465 years of Judah's history, despite the fact that he assumed leadership of a nation where idol worship was popular.

Hezekiah could have mourned over the mess he inherited, either hating his father or blaming God for the wretched moral and economic conditions that prevailed throughout the nation. Instead, Hezekiah, *in the first year of his reign ... opened the doors of the House of the LORD. ... and said to the priests and the Levites ... sanctify yourselves, and. ... make a covenant with the Lord God of Israel. ... make a proclamation throughout all Israel ... to keep the Passover. ... So there was great joy in Jerusalem* (II Chronicles 29:3-5,10; 30: 5,26). Hezekiah used the two most-powerful means given to mankind to overcome his difficulties. First, he had his heart set on returning the nation to the Word of God. When Judah was attacked by Sennacherib, king of Assyria, the most-powerful nation of that time, Hezekiah said to the people: *Be strong and courageous, be not afraid . . . with us is the LORD our God to help us, and to fight our battles* (32:7-8). **Then Hezekiah found a prayer partner, the Prophet Isaiah, and they prayed and cried to heaven.**

The king of Assyria demanded unconditional surrender. Feeling that his army was invincible, Sennacherib sent word to the people of Jerusalem: *Let not Hezekiah deceive you: for he shall not be able to deliver you. Neither let Hezekiah make you trust in the LORD, saying, The LORD will surely deliver us* (Isaiah 36:14-16).

Upon hearing this demand, King Hezekiah could have "sanctimoniously" said: "I will leave our fate in the hands of the Lord." But, he realized that **God had left it up to him to pray,** so he immediately did what we all should do when we receive bad news. *Hezekiah . . . went up to the House of the LORD. . . . And **Hezekiah prayed** . . . O LORD . . . You*

are God, even You alone, of all the kingdoms of the earth.
. . . hear all the words of Sennacherib, which (he) *has*
sent to reproach the living God. . . . save us (37:1-20).
The key to Hezekiah's prayer being answered was
his foremost desire that, through their deliverance,
all the kingdoms of the earth may know that You are the
LORD, *even You only* (37:20).

Isaiah sent a message to Hezekiah, saying: *Thus*
says the LORD *God of Israel, Because you have prayed to*
Me against Sennacherib king of Assyria. . . . I will defend
this city to save it for My own sake, and for My servant
David's sake (37:21,35). That night *the Angel of the*
LORD *went forth, and smote . . . the Assyrians* (37:36),
destroying all 185,000 of Sennacherib's soldiers.

When our situation seems hopeless, we can remember Hezekiah, pray and trust the Lord. It is
foolish to think we can *stand against the wiles*
(schemes, trickery) *of the devil* in our own might
(Ephesians 6:11). God is waiting to bless us as we
place our trust in Him. The Lord is still urging: *Call*
(pray) *to Me, and I will answer you, and show you*
great and mighty things, which you know not (Jeremiah
33:3; also Ephesians 3:20).

About 13 years had passed since Isaiah brought
Hezekiah, king of Judah, the exciting news that his

kingdom would be miraculously saved from the "invincible" armies of the Assyrian Empire. At a later time, Isaiah said to Hezekiah, who was gravely ill: *Thus says the LORD, Set your house in order: for you shall die, and not live* (Isaiah 38:1; II Kings 20:1; II Chronicles 32:24-26).

Hezekiah did not "set his house in order" but *turned his face toward the wall, and **prayed to the** LORD, And said, Remember now, O LORD, I beseech* (beg) *You, how **I have walked before You in truth and with a perfect** (sincere) **heart**, and have done that which is good in Your sight. And Hezekiah wept sore* **(bitterly)** (Isaiah 38:2-3; compare 38:17). He reminded the Lord how he had served Him faithfully. **He had sincerely lived to please the Lord.** Then Isaiah again heard the voice of God: *Go, and say to Hezekiah, **Thus says the** LORD . . . **I have heard your prayer, I have seen your tears**: behold, I will add to your days 15 years* (38:5). Surely the 15 additional years were not only due to Hezekiah's tears and prayer but to his faithfulness to the Word of God during the previous 39 years of his life.

As with Hezekiah who inherited serious problems because his father was an evil king, we too may be the victim of other people's sins. As Chris-

tians, we never need to fear the future or "unfortu-
nate circumstances" of our parents' past mistakes,
which we may have inherited, or other situations
over which we have no control. Dwelling on one's
past mistakes, or those of others, never provides
helpful solutions, and can create depression, sus-
picion, self-hatred, and hatred of others. How en-
couraging it is to know that, **when Hezekiah and
Isaiah prayed, the Lord answered their prayers.**

We should **never hesitate to pray, regardless of
how hopeless our circumstances may appear.** However, this does not mean that God always answers
every prayer in the way we desire or according to
our timing.

Since all of us fall short in our desire to be like
Jesus, some Christians find it easy to accept the
condemnation of Satan that they are too unworthy
for God to answer their prayers. Although it is important that we assess our faults and confess our
sins, it also magnifies the grace of God to recognize
the good in our lives just as Hezekiah did. We can
also remind the Lord of our sincere endeavors to
live God-honoring lives. *Not by works of righteousness which we have done, but according to His mercy He
saved us, by the washing of regeneration, and renewing*

of the Holy Spirit (Titus 3:5; also James 5:16).

Thought for the day: *Commit your way to the LORD; trust also in Him; and He shall bring it to pass* (accomplish whatever the need is) (Psalm 37:5).

I love Thee, Lord; I love Thy will.
Do Thou Thy plan through me fulfill
That glory may return to Thee
For time and for eternity.

In natural strength no honor lies;
Thy grace alone sin's power defies,
but Satan's power is nullified
Through all in whom Christ does abide.

The victory of Christ — complete —
Through all the ages stands replete
As any humble, trusting soul
Yields fully to Thy blessed control.

Manasseh

*M*anasseh, Hezekiah's son, was even more wicked than Hezekiah's father Ahaz, who had closed the Temple (II Chronicles 28:24). Manasseh *did that which was evil in the sight of the LORD, after the abominations* (detestable practices) *of the heathen. . . . And he built altars for all the host of heaven in the two courts of the House of the LORD. And he made his son pass through the fire* (meaning he threw him into a raging fire into the arms of a statue of the Canaanite god Molech as a sacrifice), *and . . . he did much wickedness in the sight of the LORD, to provoke Him to anger* (II Kings 21:2-6).

Manasseh's disregard for the Word of God resulted in his being defeated by the fierce Assyrians as a judgment from God. *The captains of the host . . . took Manasseh among the thorns* (with hooks), *and bound him with fetters, and carried him to Babylon. And when he was in affliction* (misery, suffering), **he besought (prayed fervently to)** *the LORD his God, and humbled himself greatly before . . . God . . . And prayed to Him: and He was entreated of him* (moved by his prayers) . . . *and* (God) *brought him again to Jerusalem into his kingdom. Then Manasseh knew that the* LORD *He was God* (II Chronicles 33:10-13).

As sinful as he had been, **when Manasseh repented and continued to pray, the Lord forgave him** and made it possible for him to be released as a prisoner of Assyria and to be reinstated as king of Judah. This was a miraculous answer to Manasseh's prayers for mercy and forgiveness since Assyria was known for its ruthless cruelty.

Only God knows what effect the prayers of his godly father Hezekiah many years earlier may have had on Manasseh's change of heart. God forgives even the most evil sinners when they truly repent and pray for forgiveness. Upon being restored as king, Manasseh immediately destroyed the false gods and altars he had previously built. Then he rebuilt the altar for the Temple and returned to the true worship of the Lord that had existed during the reign of his father.

But Manasseh could not relive the wasted years of his previous sinful reign nor even convince his own son to reject idols and worship the Lord. After Manasseh's death, his son Amon reinstated all the wicked, idolatrous practices of his father's earlier reign (33:22). *And he . . . served the idols . . . and worshiped them* (II Kings 21:21). This points out the irreversible law of seed time and harvest. Even though God fully forgives our sinful past, we too are warned: *Be not deceived . . . whatsoever a man sows, that shall he also reap. For he that sows to his flesh shall of the flesh reap corruption* (destruction); *but he that sows to the Spirit shall of the Spirit reap life everlasting* (Galatians 6:7-8).

Thought for the day: *The effectual fervent prayer of a righteous man avails* (accomplishes) *much* (James 5:16).

Only a day, yes, only a day
But ah! could you guess my friend,
Where the influence reaches
and where it will end
Of the hours you have frittered away?
The Master's command is, "Abide in Me."
And fruitless and vain will your service be
If you are out of touch with your Lord.

Josiah

*J*osiah's reign was remarkable: *Like to him was there no king before him, that turned to the LORD with all his heart, and with all his soul, and with all his might, according to the Law of Moses; neither after him arose there any like him* (II Kings 23:25).

In the midst of national rebellion against God, Josiah stood almost alone for God and righteousness. He didn't give in to the political pressure that opposed his spiritual values. He was not intimidated by the majority into being politically correct. Instead, he aggressively *put away the workers of familiar spirits, and the wizards, and the images, and the idols, and all the abominations that were spied in the land of Judah and in Jerusalem . . . that he might perform the words of the Law which were written in the book that Hilkiah the priest found in the House of the LORD* (23:24). These abominations had become popular throughout Judah and were widely practiced. After the evil practices had ceased, the nation was once again in a position to be blessed of God. We admire Josiah for his desire and determination to return the nation to worship the One True God.

Josiah was zealous for the Lord *and had turned to the LORD with all his heart,* but there is no mention that he prayed for God's will before going to war with the king of Egypt against the king of Assyria, who *slew him at Megiddo* (23:29). After his death, his son Jehoahaz ruled over the kingdom, and *he did that which was evil in the sight of the LORD* (23:32). The results that followed were inevitable.

Just three months later, Jehoahaz was removed from the throne and taken in chains to Egypt and his older brother Jehoiakim, who was even more wicked, reigned as king. In defiance against the prophet of God, Jehoiakim cut up and burned a copy of God's Word (see Jeremiah 36:22-23). His evil ways accelerated the Kingdom of Judah on its downward spiral to destruction.

Jehoiakim did not believe God would allow the Syrians, then the Moabites, and then the Ammonites – one nation after another – to destroy Judah's defenses. The final blow came some years later when Nebuchadnezzar destroyed Jerusalem during the reign of Jehoiakim's younger brother Zedekiah.

With everyone, both then and now, God is pleading: *If My people, which are called by My Name, shall humble themselves, and pray, and seek My face, and turn away from their wicked ways; then will I hear from heaven, and will forgive their sin, and will heal their land* (II Chronicles 7:14).

When things are going wrong, we have a tendency to point the finger of blame at someone else without recognizing that God may be using defeat after defeat to help us realize our need to repent, turn from our sinful ways, and seek the Lord.

God is merciful and longsuffering. He didn't allow Judah to be defeated by the first nation that declared war against it. Its defeat was gradual. Having failed to repent, they eventually were carried away in three stages of deportation. In their apostasy, they thought it was the surrounding nations that were against them. They never considered that God Almighty was behind the nations, moving them to attack.

Surely (Without a doubt) *at the commandment of the LORD came this upon Judah, to remove them out of His sight* (II Kings 24:3). **No prayer of repentance is recorded** during the reign of Judah's last four kings.

If we are out of the will of God, we do not have good judgment because only God – through His Word and His Holy Spirit – can impart good judgment. God will direct us when we are in submission to Him. We are urged to *trust in the LORD with all your heart, and lean not to your own understanding. In all your ways acknowledge Him, and He will direct your paths* (Proverbs 3:5-6). Since God is holy, He cannot excuse sin. Neither will He forgive our sins unless we pray for forgiveness with a sincere desire for the Lord to rule our lives (see I John 1:6-10).

God will bring His will to pass regardless of how clever we are in attempting to dodge His judgment. God is the One we will ultimately face (see Ecclesiastes 12:14). When our lives are in submission to Him, it is amazing how *all things work together for good* (Romans 8:28). When our lives are not in submission to Him, it is disturbing to see the confusion He allows in order to awaken us. He has warned: *Awake you that sleep, and arise from the* (spiritually) *dead, and Christ shall give you light. See then that you walk circumspectly* (with great care live to please Christ), *not as fools, but as wise* (Ephesians 5:14-15).

Thought for the day: The prophet wisely said: *O LORD, I know that the way of man is not in himself: it is not in man that walks to direct his steps* (Jeremiah 10:23).

Jehoshaphat

Jehoshaphat was one of the most godly kings in the history of Judah. He forced the Baal and Ashtoreth cult followers, as well as the male prostitutes (homosexuals), out of Israel. He also appointed Levites throughout his kingdom to read and instruct people in the Word of God. (See II Chronicles 17:3-9.)

However, Jehoshaphat made a serious mistake when he became friends with Ahab, the Baal-worshiping king of the northern kingdom. This led to the marriage of Jehoshaphat's son to Ahab's daughter. As is often the case, one decision made out of the will of God leads to another. Eventually Ahab requested his help in a war with Syria. Jehoshaphat must have felt obligated, so he joined Ahab in the war and would have been killed except for his fervent prayer.

When surrounded by Syrians, **Jehoshaphat cried out (prayed with all his being)**, *and the LORD helped him; and God moved them to depart from him* (II Chronicles 18:31). Then *Jehoshaphat the king of Judah re-*

turned to his house in peace to Jerusalem (19:1). **God marvelously answered his prayer**. This incident illustrates the meaning of *the effectual fervent prayer of a righteous man avails much* (James 5:16).

Fervent prayer is needed at this turbulent time in history. We can also thank the Lord for faithful Prophets like Jehu, whom God sent to rebuke Jehoshaphat: *Should you help the ungodly, and love them that hate the LORD? therefore is wrath upon you from . . . the LORD* (II Chronicles 19:2). We find it easy to forget that *friendship of the world is enmity with God* (James 4:4).

Although Jehoshaphat was a man of God, his alliance with the ungodly Ahab eventually brought about the death of all but one of his grandchildren. We need to ask ourselves: "Do I have a friend, career, or hobby standing between me and God?"

All of our relationships should be guided by the Scriptures. We have been warned: *Be not unequally yoked together with unbelievers: for what fellowship has righteousness with unrighteousness? and what communion has light with darkness? . . . come out from among them, and be separate, says the Lord* (II Corinthians 6: 14,17).

We are living in perilous times of deception and

need to be *praying always with all prayer and supplication in the Spirit, and watching thereto with all perseverance and supplication* (intense earnestness) *for all saints* (Ephesians 6:18). Jesus warned about the last generation before His return, saying: *Take heed* (Be on guard) *to yourselves, lest at any time your hearts be overcharged* (overpowered) *with surfeiting* (self-indulgence), *and drunkenness, and cares* (anxieties) *of this life . . . so that day* (of Christ's return) *come upon you unawares* (unprepared). *For as a snare* (lure) *shall it come on all them that dwell on the face of the whole earth.* **Watch . . . and pray always, that you may be accounted worthy** *to escape all these things that shall come to pass, and to stand before the Son of Man* (Jesus) (Luke 21:34-36).

The Lord expects us to receive the treasures of heaven through prayer when biblical qualifications are followed.

We are to keep in mind that *we wrestle not against flesh and blood, but against principalities, against powers, against the rulers of the darkness of this world, against spiritual wickedness in high places* (Ephesians 6:12). Never underestimate the deception of Satan, who will do all he can to discourage, distract, defeat, and prevent answers to your prayers. But, *you are of God, little children, and have overcome them* (demonic spirits): *because greater is He* (the Holy Spirit) *that is in you, than he* (Satan) *that is in the world* (I John 4:4).

We need to encourage others to be prepared for the Lord's return and do what we can to persuade a prayer partner or a group of friends to meet weekly to pray and study His Word.

Reading all the Word of God reflects our desire to hear what God has to say, how He would have us to live, and how we should pray. His Word is our weapon to use against the forces of hell, for it is *the Sword of the Spirit* (Ephesians 6:17).

We give thanks to God and the Father of our Lord Jesus Christ, **praying always for you, since we heard of your faith in Christ Jesus.** *... For this cause* **we also do not cease to pray for you,** *and to desire that you might be filled with the knowledge of His will in all wisdom and spiritual understanding* (Colossians 1:3-4,9).

Thought for the day: *Not forsaking the assembling of yourselves together, as the manner of some is; but exhorting one another: and so much the more, as you see the day approaching* (Hebrews 10:25).

Ezra

Because Ezra knew the Scriptures, the Lord could use this godly man to lead about five thousand men, women, and children on the treacherous, 800-mile journey from Babylon to Jerusalem. Added to his concern for the people was the responsibility for the priceless treasures of *silver, and the gold, and the vessels . . . of the House of . . . God, which the king . . . had offered* (Ezra 8:25). These Temple treasures had been taken by King Nebuchadnezzar when he had destroyed the *House of God* (see II Kings 24:17 – 25:17).

It would have been much easier for Ezra, as well as for the people, to remain in Babylon and **just pray for the people who remained in Jerusalem**. Ezra was fully aware of the danger of bandits who could murder and plunder. Added to this concern, the people would face both physical and emotional hardships.

In spite of all the possible problems, Ezra did not ask the king for a protective military guard. Rather, it is recorded that **Ezra *proclaimed a fast (and prayer)***. He records he did so *that we might af-*

flict (humble) *ourselves before our God, to seek of Him a right way. . . . I was ashamed to require of the king a band of soldiers . . . to help us against the enemy in the way: because we had spoken to the king, saying, The hand of our God is upon all them for good that seek Him* (8:21-22). With no tangible assurance of what the future held, Ezra decided to **fast and pray and trust the Lord.**

About four months after leaving Babylon, Ezra and all his followers arrived safely in Jerusalem (7:8-9; 8:31-32). Upon his arrival, Ezra was grief-stricken when he learned of the low moral and spiritual condition that had developed among the Israelites in Jerusalem since the Temple had been rebuilt. Ezra was told: *The people of Israel, and the priests, and the Levites, have not separated themselves from the people* (pagan idol worshipers) *of the lands, doing according to their abominations* (numerous sins) (9:1). When confronted with the great need, he did not say: "It's not my problem, so I'll leave it up to someone else." Instead, he became involved and identified himself with the people in a prayer of repentance and *every one that trembled at the words of the God of Israel* (9:4) assembled before him.

At the evening sacrifice, Ezra fell on his knees and spread out his hands to the Lord, and **prayed:**

85

O my God, I am ashamed . . . for our iniquities. . . . for **we have forsaken Your Commandments** (9:6,10). The effect of one godly person praying with sincerity was immediately evident. *Now when **Ezra had prayed, and when he had confessed, weeping and casting himself down before the House of God**, there assembled to him out of Israel a very great congregation of men and women and children: for the people wept very sore* (with genuine repentance) (10:1).

Are we as concerned as Ezra about the low moral and spiritual conditions that surrounds us?

The Prophet Ezra is an example of the same power we have in prayer once we recognize the importance of obedience to the Word of God. May we be like him with our hearts broken by the things that break the heart of God.

Thought for the day: *He* (Jesus) *called to Him the twelve, and began to send them forth by two and two; and gave them power over unclean spirits. . . . And they went out, and preached that men should repent* (Mark 6:7-12).

Nehemiah

When Nehemiah's relative Hanani arrived in Persia from Jerusalem, he told Nehemiah of the pitiful conditions that existed there. Nehemiah was heartbroken when he received a report of the spiritual and physical poverty that existed in Jerusalem. The walls had remained in ruins since Nebuchadnezzar had destroyed Jerusalem about 140 years earlier (II Kings 25:8-11). The Jewish remnant had no protection from surrounding nations. They could easily come in and rob them of their harvests and possessions.

When Nehemiah was told of the pitiful situation in Jerusalem he *sat down and wept, and mourned certain days, and fasted, and prayed before the God of heaven. . . . both I and my father's house have sinned. . . . and have not kept the Commandments* (Nehemiah 1:4,6-7). Over a period of about four months, **he continued to pray**.

When King Artaxerxes asked why he was so sad, Nehemiah told him that it was because *the city, the place of my fathers' sepulchers* (tombs), *lies waste* (2:1-3). The king graciously responded by appointing him governor over Judah and commissioning him to rebuild the walls of Jerusalem. The king even provided some of the materials (2:6-8).

This was about 100 years after Zerubbabel had arrived in Jerusalem to rebuild the Temple (Ezra 1:5; 3:1) and about 14 years after Ezra had gone to Jerusalem to restore the Temple and its worship (7:6).

Three basic characteristics made Nehemiah's efforts successful. First, he desired to do the will of God (Nehemiah 1:11). This led him to leave the luxury and security of living in the king's palace in Persia and to endure the hardships in Jerusalem in order to restore the city of God.

Second, **he not only *fasted and prayed*, but he** confessed: *We. . . . have not kept the Commandments* (1:4-11). **He recognized that obedience to the Word of God is essential to answered prayer.**

Third, he was determined to persuade his people to join him in rebuilding the walls, regardless of opposition. Sanballat and his crowd immediately expressed their hostility to Nehemiah: *They laughed us to scorn, and despised us* (2:19). Their ridicule then turned to slander: *Will you rebel against the king?* To make the situation even more difficult for

Nehemiah, Judah's *nobles* (chief leaders) *put not their necks to the work* (would not cooperate in building the wall) (3:5). But, ridicule and loss of popularity will never intimidate those who know that God hears and answers prayer.

Eleven times it is recorded that Nehemiah prayed (1:4-11; 2:4; 4:4-5,9; 5:19; 6:9,14; 13:14,22,29, 31). He had no doubt that God would answer his prayers. With the utmost confidence, he encouraged the workers, saying: *The God of heaven . . . will prosper us* (2:20). Because *the people had a mind to work. . . . the wall was finished . . . in fifty and two days* (4:6; 6:15).

Although faced with numerous problems (Nehemiah 4:12-23; 6:2-4,10-13), a revival took place among the people because of their **continual prayer and fasting** (8:2,8,12).

Nehemiah refused to become discouraged and give up. Quitters never win and winners never quit. Accomplishing the will of God is dependent upon remembering that without exception He is Sovereign over our lives.

Once we recognize *the battle is the LORD's* (I Samuel 17:47) and that God is the One who allows the opposition, we will **continue to pray** as well as to do what we can to bring the Lord's will to pass. We will also seek to learn what the Lord expects from us in order to qualify and have our prayers answered. People of faith, though a minority, will always find a way to accomplish God's will.

In serving the Lord, one temptation many Christians face is to make excuses to wait for a more convenient time to pray rather than to put the Lord first and do their best with what they have. May Nehemiah's faithfulness be our example. *The God of heaven, He will prosper us* (Nehemiah 2:20).

Thought for the day: *Teach me Your way, O LORD; I will walk in Your truth: unite my heart to fear* (revere) *Your Name* (Psalm 86:11).

In Jesus' Name, I hide me still
For there alone the Father's will
Can be determined, or made known,
To all who seek His gracious Throne.

All efforts of the flesh are vain,
In Christ alone we must remain
And Thus approach the Throne of Grace
To seek the Heavenly Father's face.

Job Prayed

*J*ob suffered financial hardship, emotional tribulation, and painful physical trials. Like some people today, Job's friends were of the opinion that if a person is godly, he will not suffer or have any problems – and that all sickness is the result of sin.

In contrast, God said that Job was a righteous man five times – the biblical number for mercy and grace. But God allowed Job to endure extreme suffering. He lost all ten children, all his cattle, and his servants in one day. His wife also told Job that he should curse God and die. All of Job's friends told him that the reason he was suffering was because he was a sinful man. However, Job's pitiful, painful condition was not because of a sinful life, but because he was the most godly man on earth. God knew that He could depend on Job to reveal to the world that righteous people do suffer and, that through suffering, their faith would draw them into a closer relationship with God. Job's response to critics concerning his suffering was that *the LORD gave, and the LORD has taken away; blessed be the Name of the* LORD *(1:21). He knows the way that I take: when He has tried me, I shall come forth as gold (23:10).* **The key to Job's remarkable faith** is revealed in his seventh response to his critics when he said: *His way have I kept. . . . Neither have I gone back from the commandment of His lips;* **I have esteemed the words of His mouth more** (more important) *than my necessary food (23:11-12).*

Through a series of more than 80 questions, God revealed to Job many wonders of the universe, some of which have only recently been "discovered" by scientists. Because of his faith in God and his patience through suffering, Job acknowledged the supreme authority of God compared to how little is known by mankind. It is no surprise to read that **Job prayed**: *I know that You can do every thing, and that no thought can be withheld from You. . . . I uttered that I understood not; things too wonderful for me, which I knew not (42:2-3).* By this he meant: "Although I did not understand, I will never question what God does or what He allows to happen, since His love and wisdom are perfect."

Our limited knowledge and ability to cope with life's problems should cause all of us to be reminded that **God is waiting for our prayers** and has promised: *If any of you lack wisdom, let him ask of* (pray to) *God, that gives to all men liberally, and upbraids* (reproaches, scolds) *not; and it shall be given him* (James 1:5). How foolish it is to question the wisdom and love of God for His children! We need to accept, with submissive hearts, the circumstances He allows in our lives and which He chooses to use to fulfill His loving, eternal purposes. During times of personal afflictions, heartbreaking bereavement, persecution, or financial struggles, some may become bitter or depressed and even fail to pray because of their lack of faith. That is when we need the loving comfort and assurance that **our Heavenly Father** ultimately **controls every situation** that comes into our lives. Peter encouraged Christians when he wrote: *Casting all your care* (anxiety and fear) *upon Him; for **He cares for you*** (I Peter 5:7). Regardless of how hopeless our situation may seem, our Heavenly Father wants to use our trials for our good and for His glory (see Romans 8:28; also Genesis 50:20). This means that we need to *continue in prayer, and watch in the same with thanksgiving* (Colossians 4:2).

During his suffering, Job experienced glorious revelations of the incomparable greatness of God and His ways. Job's spiritual understanding continued to grow day by day through his suffering, and he prayed: *I have heard of You by the hearing of the ear: but now my eye sees You. Wherefore I abhor myself, and repent in dust and ashes* (Job 42:5-6). Those who trust in the Lord, as Job did, are not desperately searching for the answers to all of life's problems, nor asking the questions: "Why?" or "Why me?" They are simply trusting our loving, all-wise Father, who always knows what we need and will give His best to those who trust Him. Praise the Lord!

God personally visited Job's friends and rebuked them for abusing His servant Job. They must have been astounded to hear the Voice from heaven say to Eliphaz: *My wrath is kindled against you, and against your two friends: for you have not spoken of Me the thing that is right, as My servant Job has* (42:7). God also told them to go to His servant Job **that he might pray for them**. If it hadn't been for Job's suffering, his friends would never have known that they needed to be prayed for to be in a right relationship with God. Job could have become proud after God came to his defense. Instead, **he humbly prayed for God to forgive his three friends** who had so cruelly criticized him. *And the LORD* turned the captivity of Job, when he prayed for his friends (42:10).

Jesus also was our example when He commanded His disciples: *Bless them that curse you, and pray for them which despitefully use you* (Luke 6:28). **Forgiving our enemies and praying for them is an indispensable key to answered prayer.**

Thought for the day: Let's follow the example of the Apostle Paul, who said: *Not that I speak in respect of want . . . I have learned, in whatsoever state* (circumstances) *I am, therewith to be content. I know both how to be abased* (to live victoriously when things are difficult), *and I know how to abound* (what it is like to have all I need) (Philippians 4:11-12).

Trust in the Lord with all thine heart
Nor ever from His Word depart,
Then thou wilt be most blest indeed
In thought and word, as well as deed.

Without His blessing all is loss —
No word of comfort from the Cross,
The Holy Ghost, and He alone
Can work God's will within His own.

David's Confession ~ Psalm 51

$\mathcal{D}$avid disregarded the Word of God on the day he coveted the beautiful wife of one of his most loyal soldiers. While Uriah the Hittite was at war, David committed adultery with his wife. Then, in an attempt to conceal his sin and legally marry Bathsheba, he arranged to have Uriah in the front line of a battle where he was killed.

It appeared to be a happy ending for David and Bathsheba, but only for about one year. After the birth of their child, God sent Nathan, a friend of King David and a fearless prophet of God, to denounce the king's wicked sins. Nathan first told David that a rich man who had many herds and flocks robbed a poor man of his only lamb and then killed it for his feast. David was very angry that a man could be so cruel and said the man should be put to death. Nathan responded: *You are the man. Thus says the LORD God of Israel, I anointed you king over Israel, and I delivered you out of the hand of Saul; And I gave you your master's . . . wives . . . and gave you the house* (the kingdoms) *of Israel and of Judah. . . .*

Wherefore have you despised the Commandment of the LORD, *to do evil in His sight? You have killed Uriah the Hittite with the sword, and have taken his wife to be your wife, and have slain him with the sword of the children of Ammon. Now therefore the sword shall never depart from your house; because you have despised Me* (II Samuel 12:1,7-10).

The acts of adultery and murder were two very serious sins. They were forbidden under the Mosaic Law of God that stated: *Thou shalt not kill* (commit murder). *Thou shalt not commit adultery* (Exodus 20:13-14). *The man that commits adultery . . . shall surely be put to death. . . . you shall be holy to Me: for I . . . have severed* (separated) *you from other people, that you should be Mine* (Leviticus 20:10,26).

It was only after the Prophet Nathan reprimanded David that he faced the fact of how evil he had been as well as having been unfaithful to God, whom he represented as king over Israel. Convicted in his heart of his selfish sins, David recorded how he cast himself on the mercy of God as **a brokenhearted sinner and humbly prayed**: *Have mercy on me, O God, according to Your lovingkindness. . . . wash me thoroughly from my iniquity, and cleanse me from my sin* (I have sinned against the Lord).

For I acknowledge my transgressions: and my sin is ever before me. Against You, You only, have I sinned, and done this evil in Your sight. . . . Create in me a clean heart, O God; and renew a right spirit within me (Psalm 51:1-4,10; see also verses 5-19).

It was sin that separated David from God, and he rightly called it *iniquity* and sin against the holy and righteous God. The Holy Spirit led David to record his own prayer of sorrow and repentance. It allows us to see by his example that God is merciful to **all repentant sinners**. After **his long prayer of repentance** recorded in Psalm 51, *Nathan said to David, the* LORD *. . . has put away your sin; you shall not die* (II Samuel 12:13).

In answer to David's sincere prayer, God forgave him. But, Nathan also reminded David that by his sins, he had *given great occasion to the enemies of the* LORD *to blaspheme* (show utter contempt) (II Samuel 12:13-14). For David, his sin resulted in personal shame and suffering for the rest of his life, as well as many tragic personal and national consequences.

We wish that this blight upon David's life had not happened. However, it was recorded not only to reveal the deception and never-ending devastation of lust, but also to let us know that God forgives us when we repent, forsake our sins, and **pray as David did**. This gives hope to all of us who truly repent of our sins that we can experience the same mercy and forgiving love of God. **David's repentance and his prayer for mercy released him from the penalty of his sins**, but not from the consequences of those sins (see 12:10). No one can escape the emotional, social, financial, and, certainly, spiritual grief and shame caused by his sins.

David did not pray that he would not suffer consequences of his sin. In fact, during the last 20 years of his life he suffered many tragedies as a result of his sin. It is an inescapable law of nature that *whatever a man sows, that shall he also reap* (Galatians 6:7).

Recognizing our need for **God's mercy is an important key to acceptable prayer**. Think of it, without the mercy of God we would all be eternally lost. David's prayer was inspired by the Holy Spirit and recorded to let us know **how to pray** to be forgiven of our sins. It also assures us that if we pray as David did, we will be forgiven of our sins as a result of genuine repentance. *If we confess our sins, He is faithful and just to forgive us our sins, and to cleanse us from all unrighteousness* (I John 1:9). *He that* *covers his sins shall not prosper: but whoso confesses and forsakes them shall have mercy* (Proverbs 28:13). While mercy may lighten a person's sentence, forgiveness pardons the one who committed the sin and takes away sin's sentence of death; but it does not remove the consequences of sin.

There are three inescapable facts that we must face if our **prayers are to be answered** and we are to have a right relationship with God:

1. We need to recognize how grievous sin is to God, who is holy;

2. We must forsake sin and pray for forgiveness;

3. We must live in sincere, heartfelt thankfulness to God for His mercy and forgiveness.

David could have blamed Bathsheba for bathing in an open area and causing him to be tempted. David was the king, and kings usually assume final authority over their subjects. He could have said that he had served God from his youth. After all, he had killed the giant Goliath and won the war against the Philistines. He had held no hatred for Saul. He never worshiped idols. He could have defended himself, saying: "So, I made a mistake." But, David offered no excuses.

The sincerely repentant sinner, like David, will

quickly acknowledge full responsibility for his sin. Some try to justify their sin by saying: "But it was somebody else's fault", "Everybody does it", or "I grew up in a bad environment, etc. etc." **David cried (prayed):** *My sin is ever before me* (Psalm 51:3).

Genuine repentance is a confession that we have violated and broken God's sacred Law by refusing to do what He has commanded. If we truly regret our sin, we will genuinely repent.

Many people are deceived. They want to get answers to their prayers, but they are not willing to abandon their sins.

When we excuse ourselves, sin blinds the heart and causes pride, which makes a sinner unwilling to humble himself. Without exception, we are all sinners and deserve to be *cast into the lake of fire* (for eternity) (Revelation 20:15). But the marvelous mercy of God makes the difference. Jesus has promised: *Him that comes to Me I will in no wise cast out* (John 6:37).

We are commanded to *present* (our) *bodies a living sacrifice, holy, acceptable to God, which is* (our) *reasonable service* (Romans 12:1). We are also required to *be not conformed to this world: but be transformed by the renewing of our mind, that we may prove* (discover) *what is that good, and acceptable, and perfect, will of God* (12:2).

This involves *bringing into captivity every thought to the obedience of Christ* (II Corinthians 10:5). Also, we are to *have no fellowship with the unfruitful works of darkness, but rather reprove* (seek to correct) *them* (Ephesians 5:11).

David began his prayer for *mercy* for himself; but the longer he prayed, the more his prayer became intercession for a needy world. David continued his prayer with a promise: *I will teach transgressors Your ways; and sinners shall be converted* (Psalm 51:13). When one has experienced the *mercy* of God, he has a desire to share with others his personal cleansing from sin and the overwhelming enjoyment of being forgiven. David also poured out his heart: *LORD, open . . . my lips; and my mouth shall show forth Your praise* (51:15).

Thought for the day: The Holy Spirit led Luke to record the parable of a publican who prayed in the Temple: *God be merciful to me a sinner. . . this man went down to his house justified* (Luke 18:13-14). *Blessed is he whose transgression is forgiven, whose sin is covered* (Psalm 32:1).

David's Prayer of Praise

*D*avid was forced to flee to a desolate area out-side of the promised land because of Saul's relent-less efforts to kill him. Even after ten years of being exiled from his loved ones, from the physical com-forts of the palace, and most of all from the place of worship, David never lost faith in God. He prayed: *Hear my cry, O God: attend* (listen) *to my prayer. From the end of the earth I will cry to You, when my heart is overwhelmed: lead me to the Rock that is higher than I. For you have been a shelter for me, and a strong tower from the enemy* (Psalm 61:1-3).

After more than 10 years of being hunted by Saul, the day came when the Philistines attacked the Israelites, and King Saul and his sons were slain in battle. An Amalekite nomad, who stole the crown of Saul, mistakenly thought David would be delighted when he claimed that he had executed Saul. The Amalekite could not imagine David not rejoicing over the death of his cruel enemy. But, David *mourned, and wept, and fasted until evening ... because they* (Saul and his sons) *were fallen by the sword.... And David lamented.... The beauty of Israel is slain upon your high places: how are the mighty fallen! Tell it not in Gath, publish it not in the streets of Askelon; lest the daughters of the Philistines rejoice* (II Samuel 1:12,17,19-20).

The world delights in the failures of Christians. Surely no Christian should ever be involved in gossip about the failures of fellow Christians. *If any man among you seem to be religious* (God-fearing), *and bridles* (controls) *not his tongue, but deceives his own heart, this man's religion is vain* (worthless) (James 1:26), and obviously his prayers go unanswered.

Now that Saul was dead, who would reign in his place? Israel was without a king. David had been anointed long ago by Samuel the prophet to be king of the Israelite kingdom (I Samuel 16:1-13). However, Abner, Saul's cousin and the powerful commander of Saul's army, was determined to retain his position. He persuaded the elders of Israel to put Saul's crippled and helpless son Ish-bosheth on the throne to rule over the 10 tribes. David could have felt justified in challenging Abner in battle and fighting for his right as God's chosen successor. Instead, *David inquired of* **(prayed to)** *the* Lord, *saying, Shall I go up into any of the cities of Judah? And* the LORD *said to him, Go up. And David prayed, Where shall I go up? And He said, To Hebron.... And the men of* (the one tribe of) *Judah came, and there they anointed David king over the house of Judah* (II Samuel 2:1,4).

How prone we are to jump at every opportunity for personal advancement rather than to pray for His will for our lives! David illustrates **the importance of praying for God's will to be done** in His way and at His time. Spiritual victory is not dependent on human strength or reasoning but on **prayer and submission to the Holy Spirit**.

Near the end of his life, David could say: *I have kept the ways of the LORD, and have not wickedly departed from my God.... With the merciful You will show Yourself merciful, and with the upright man You will show Yourself upright.... And the afflicted people You will save: but Your eyes are upon the haughty, that You may bring them down.... As for God, His way is perfect; the Word of the LORD is tried* (never fails): *He is a buckler* (protector, shield) *to all them that trust in Him.... The LORD lives; and blessed be my Rock; and exalted be the God of my salvation.... Therefore, I will* (pray and) *give thanks to You, O LORD, among the heathen* (nations), *and I will sing praises to Your Name* (22:22,26,28,31,47,50).

This is a song that the Holy Spirit led David to pray that we need to read many times, **meditate, and pray that we too will be *a man* (or woman) *after God's own heart*** (I Samuel 13:14). In this prayer we are impressed with David's praise to the Lord for everything that God had provided. In contrast, how often we wait to pray until evil things are confronting us, when the opposition is assailing us, or when it looks like we can't get through the day. Yes, **the Lord is waiting for our prayer of praise** that we too will be *delivered . . . out of the hand of all . . . enemies* (II Samuel 22:1). God is waiting for us to praise Him when everything goes as expected but also when things don't go well! That's genuine praise! God loves to see us grateful for giving us the privilege of being His children, and for ALL He has given us. God gave us what He knew was best. *God is no respecter of persons* (Acts 10:34).

We should always thank the Lord for the privilege we have every day to praise Him, to pray that we will *bring into captivity every thought to the obedience of Christ* (II Corinthians 10:5), and to *present our bodies a living sacrifice, holy, acceptable to God, which is our reasonable service* (Romans 12:1). We would be mistaken to expect everything to be pleasant! Like

David, God may bring a Saul into our lives to test us and mature us for greater usefulness in His Kingdom. It's wonderful knowing that we can trust *the LORD to deliver us out of the hand of all our enemies* when He has accomplished His purpose. In fact, we can count on it since God *is the same yesterday, and to day, and for ever* (Hebrews 13:8).

When the waves of death compassed me, the floods of ungodly men made me afraid. Like David, we can expect at times *waves* (furious billows of troubles that appear to overwhelm us) (II Samuel 22:5).

All of us will face death and often sooner than expected. But, the difference between believers in Christ as Savior and Lord and the unbelieving world which faces His fierce judgment is the peace we have in knowing where we will be after death. As Christians, we have the utmost confidence that we *will dwell in the house of the LORD for ever* (Psalm 23:5).

Thought for the day: *Oh that men would praise the LORD for His goodness, and for His wonderful works to the children of men* (Psalm 107:8,15,21,31).

Isaiah Prayed

During Isaiah's time, the Word of God, as proclaimed by Isaiah, had been ignored by the Israelites. Finally, God recounted through him these heartrending words: *I have spread out My hands all the day to a rebellious people, which walked in a way that was not good, after their own thoughts* (Isaiah 65:2). Although God repeatedly had reached out to them in love, they had gone their own ways. The consequences were inevitable. The Lord continued: *I . . . will choose their delusions, and will bring their fears* (dread, terrors) *upon them; because when I called, none did answer; when I spoke, they did not hear: but they did evil before My eyes, and chose that in which I delighted not* (66:4).

To the small minority who remained faithful then, as well as to the faithful today, the Lord, through Isaiah, is saying: *Hear the Word of the* LORD, **you that tremble at His Word**; *Your brethren that hated* (despised) *you, that cast you out for My Name's sake . . . shall be ashamed. . . . For thus says the* LORD, *Behold, I will extend peace . . . like a river* (66:5,12).

During Isaiah's time, the Israelite leaders had complained to God: *Why have we fasted* (**fasting always included prayer**) *. . . and You see not? why have we afflicted our soul, and You take no knowledge?* – meaning: "Why don't You answer our prayers?" (58:3). **They accused God of not paying attention to their prayers**, and they felt He was unjust. The Lord doesn't always give us what we ask for, even when it seems to us there is no alternative answer. In fact, at times it appears He doesn't even hear us. What then are we to do?

The Lord answered: *In the day of your fast you find pleasure* (continue to seek selfish interests), *and exact* (exploit) *all your labors* (laborers). *. . . you fast for* (continue your) *strife and debate, and to smite with the fist of wickedness* (you are occupied with personal conflicts and sinful attitudes) (58:3-4).

Even more serious than their attitude was their hypocrisy. The Lord replied by questioning them: *Is it such a fast that I have chosen? a day for a man to afflict his soul* (attempt to attract God's attention)*? is it to bow down his head as a bulrush, and to spread sackcloth and ashes under him* (to impress others with pretended humility)*?* (58:5; also Luke 18:10-14).

Through Isaiah, God reminded the Israelites

that **acceptable prayer and fasting were not in-tended to impress the world** about how religious they were. The Lord said the fast that He would accept would be preceded by attitudes of goodwill and kindness such as *to loose the bands* (bonds) *of wickedness, to undo the heavy burdens, and to let the oppressed go free.* He further declared it was *to deal* (share) *your bread with the hungry, and that you bring the poor that are cast out* (wandering) *to your house. . . . when you see the naked, that you cover him; and that you hide not yourself from your own flesh* (never ne-glect your responsibility to the needs of your own family) (Isaiah 58:6-7).

The Apostle Paul quoted from Isaiah 64:4 to reveal to the Corinthian church **the power of prayer.** He wrote: *As it is written, Eye has not seen, nor ear heard, neither have entered into the heart of man, the things which God has prepared for them that love Him* (I Corinthians 2:9). The magnificence of God's wis-dom and glory are now revealed to us as we read His Word. Paul went on to state that believers in Jesus also receive the very *mind of Christ* (2:10-16) through the written Word of God.

We have become *sons of God . . . Which were born . . . of God* (John 1:12-13). **At any time**, in any place,

we may pray to our loving Heavenly Father. While we have an opportunity to serve Him, we should determine to make His will the highest priority in our lives.

It's possible that our prayer does not bring glory or honor to God or that some sin may stand between us and the fulfillment of our desired request. The psalmist was led to write: *If I regard iniquity* (wickedness) *in my heart, the Lord will not hear me* (Psalm 66:18).

Another hindrance to answered prayer could be that we pray for the right thing but have an ulterior motive. If what we do for someone (or for the Lord) is done with the hope of **expecting special favors in return, prayers and fasting will be futile**. Our prayers are effective only when our attitude and our relationship with others express the mercy and love of God.

Wrong motives may also be hindrances to answered prayer. For example, if you are praying for a friend or family member to be saved, you are praying for something that is according to His will (see II Peter 3:9). But why do you want that person saved? Is there a self-centered motive such as to make a better marriage partner or to make a home more compatible? Everyone's salvation should be desired first and foremost because they live in rebellion against God, are captives of Satan, and will be eternally lost if they do not accept Christ as their Savior.

If we ask any petition merely to receive something for our own pleasure or personal gratification, perhaps we *ask amiss* because it would be a self-serving request. We need to remember that the foremost purpose in prayer should be that God may be glorified in the answer. To illustrate this, the Scriptures record how the Israelites were out of the will of God when they expressed dissatisfaction with God's provisions of manna and complained: *We remember the fish, which we did eat in Egypt freely; the cucumbers, and the melons, and the leeks . . . and the garlic: But now our soul is dried away: there is nothing at all, beside this manna* (Numbers 11:5-6). *And the* LORD *smote* (struck) *the people with a very great plague* (11:31-33). *And when the people complained, it displeased the* LORD *. . . and His anger was kindled; and the fire of the* LORD *. . . consumed them. . . . and when Moses prayed to the* LORD, *the fire was quenched* (11:1-2).

Repeatedly, when the Israelites took God's love

and mercy for granted, they became ungrateful and rebellious, as if God should respond to their every desire. An attitude of gratitude is vital in our relationship with God.

Jesus expressed His disappointment when only one leper returned to praise and thank Him when He had healed ten lepers. He asked: *Were there not ten cleansed? but where are the nine?* (Luke 17:17).

We are given another reminder to express gratitude as we read how the disciples in the early church *were continually in the Temple, praising and blessing God* (24:53). In contrast is the one who complains instead of expressing gratitude and *abounding therein with thanksgiving* (Colossians 2:7; see also Philippians 4:6).

When we approach God in prayer with a request, we should always thank our Father in heaven for all the blessings we have already received from Him. He loves to hear our heartfelt: **"Thank You, Lord,"** as the psalmist was led to write: *Offer to God thanksgiving; and pay your vows to the Most High: And call upon Me in the day of trouble: I will deliver you, and you shall glorify Me* (Psalm 50:14-15).

We can trust God the Father as to what the best answer to our prayer is since we *know not what we should pray for as we ought; but the Spirit Himself makes intercession for us* (Romans 8:26).

The Apostle Paul was in prison at Rome because he believed and taught that Jesus was the fulfillment of all prophecy in the Old Testament concerning the Messiah. He had founded a church in Philippi on his second missionary journey, and while in prison he was led to remind them: *Be careful for* (worry about) *nothing; but **in every thing by prayer and supplication with thanksgiving** let your requests be made known to God* (Philippians 4:6).

Never underestimate the power of the Holy Spirit in bringing about answers to prayer. We are to be *praying always with all prayer and supplication in the Spirit* (Ephesians 6:18). God the Father answers the prayer that God the Holy Spirit inspires.

Thought for the day: Thanksgiving in our prayer life results in many blessings, *and the peace of God, which passes all understanding, shall keep your hearts and minds through Christ Jesus* (Philippians 4:7).

Zedekiah

Zedekiah, the last king of Judah, failed to sincerely pray during the eleven years of his evil reign. When the armies of Nebuchadnezzar surrounded Jerusalem, Zedekiah frantically requested of Jeremiah: *Inquire . . . of the Lord for us; for Nebuchadnezzar . . . makes war against us* (Jeremiah 21:2). But the answer from the Lord was firm: *I have set My face against this city for evil . . . the king of Babylon . . . shall burn it with fire* (21:10). This was because neither Zedekiah *nor the people of the land, did hearken* (listen) *to the words of the Lord, which He spoke by the Prophet Jeremiah* (37:2).

Instead of repenting of his sins and praying for the will of God, Zedekiah assumed that Egypt would protect his kingdom, so he sent his officials to Egypt to make an alliance. Because it also seemed politically wise to show "good will" to the prophet, *Zedekiah the king sent . . . the priest to the Prophet Jeremiah, saying,* **Pray now to the Lord our God for us** (37:3). The only interest Zedekiah and the Israelites had in prayer was what God could do for them. They had no thought of *humbling themselves, and praying, and seeking His face* (II Chronicles 7:14). Instead of praying, Jeremiah replied: *Thus says the* LORD; *Deceive not yourselves . . . The Chaldeans shall. . . . burn this city with fire* (Jeremiah 37:9-10).

When the Chaldean army retreated from Jerusalem, King Zedekiah believed his alliance with Egypt had been successful without the good will of the prophet. Yet Zedekiah was uneasy. Although he himself was ungodly, Zedekiah recognized that godly Jeremiah had power with God. Therefore, he removed Jeremiah from prison *and the king asked him secretly in his house . . . Is there any word from the* LORD? *And Jeremiah said, There is . . . you shall be delivered into the hand of the king of Babylon* (37:17).

A basic principle of prayer is stated in the New Testament: *Be not deceived; God is not mocked: for whatever a man sows, that shall he also reap* (Galatians 6:7).

The fortified city of Jerusalem held out for nearly a year and a half. During this time the people suffered the horrors of famine, pestilence, and even cannibalism. When Zedekiah finally attempted to escape the city at night, he was captured near Jericho, where Joshua had victoriously begun the conquest of the promised land hundreds of years earlier (Jeremiah 39:5).

After being forced to watch as his sons were murdered, Zedekiah was blinded, taken to Babylon, and imprisoned (39:7). He is an example of the pitiful consequences of those who are expecting God to answer their prayers while they refuse to repent and seek the Lord's forgiveness for their sins. A person who rejects the Lord and His Word is blindly moving toward his own eternal destruction. Regarding those, the Apostle Paul wrote: *The god of this world* (Satan) *has blinded the minds of them which believe not* (II Corinthians 4:4).

God allowed Nebuchadnezzar to defeat Zedekiah and the rebellious Israelites and fulfill His prophecy of the destruction of His once-sacred Temple and the Holy City of Jerusalem. *The king of Babylon . . . made Gedaliah . . . governor in the land, and . . . committed to him . . . them that were not carried away captive to Babylon* (Jeremiah 40:7).

Gedaliah set up his government at Mizpah, about five miles northwest of the ruins of Jerusalem. He then held a banquet in honor of Ishmael at Mizpah. Ishmael was a leader of an anti-Babylonian nationalist party. At this event, Ishmael and his ten companions murdered Gedaliah (II Kings 25:25;

Jeremiah 40:7 – 41:18). The Israelites who remained in the land evidently expected Nebuchadnezzar to retaliate, so they escaped into Egypt, forcing Jeremiah to go with them.

In Egypt, Jeremiah watched the Israelites sink further into sin as they worshiped the Egyptian goddess Ashtoreth. When confronted with their sins by the prophet, they *answered Jeremiah, saying, As for the word that you have spoken to us in the Name of the LORD, we will not hearken to you. . . . we will . . . burn incense to* (sacrifice to and worship) *the queen of heaven* (44:15-17). Because of their sins and rejection of the Word of God, faith in the living God no longer existed among these Israelites. Like so many today, they distorted the facts to fit their decision and said to Jeremiah that in Egypt we *had plenty of victuals, and were well, and saw no evil. But since we left off to burn incense to the queen of heaven . . . we have wanted* (lacked) *all things* (44:17-19).

Some would say the godly Prophet Jeremiah surely deserved better treatment than forced exile for his loyalty to the Lord. However, though distressed over the unbelief of his people, Jeremiah had nothing to fear. He knew his life was in the hands of the living God. Jeremiah never compromised; he remained loyal to God, regardless of the consequences. Centuries have passed, and you can be sure that in heaven Jeremiah has no regrets.

Thought for the day: May it also be our desire to say with God's servant, the Apostle Paul: *I count all things but loss for the excellency of the knowledge of Christ Jesus my Lord* (Philippians 3:8).

Oh! God, we lift our hearts to Thee
In contrite, humble, earnest cry
Thy Word alone, our 'stay' shall be
As on Thy wisdom we rely.

We trust Thy mercy, love and care
To sweep away all sense of doubt;
Assure our hearts of answered prayer
That Thou wilt gently lead us out.

Our trust is in our Lord Dividne
Our access by His blood alone —
All glory, honor shall be Thine
As we approach Thy sacred Throne.

Jeremiah

The powerful kingdom of Babylon was defeated and destroyed as the prophet foretold (see Jeremiah 25:12-13). However, before its destruction, Babylon was used of God to correct His people who were unfaithful to Him. The northern kingdom of Israel had been destroyed about 100 years earlier by the Assyrians who, in turn, were defeated by Nebuchadnezzar, the powerful Babylonian conquerer. This world empire then destroyed the world-famous Temple and the Holy City of Jerusalem. Jeremiah prophesied not only the captivity of the small kingdom of Judah but also its future restoration. *Thus says the LORD; Behold, I will bring again the captivity of Jacob's tents, and have mercy on his dwellingplaces; and the city shall be built upon her own heap* (ruin) (30:18).

The Prophet Jeremiah continued to warn of Israel's sin and, in response, Judah's king and religious leaders expressed a growing hatred for him. Because of their sins and continued unfaithfulness to God they had reached a point where God revealed to Jeremiah it was **too late to pray** that Jerusalem be spared from destruction (see Jeremiah 11:14; 14:11-12). Meanwhile, in Babylon, Ezekiel also recorded *that certain of the elders of Israel came to inquire* **(pray for guidance)** *of the* LORD, *and sat before me* (Ezekiel 20:1); but the Lord responded: *I will not be inquired of by you* (20:3). They were concerned about their future security but not about their spiritual failure.

During their Babylonian captivity, the Lord, through His Prophet Jeremiah, taught the Israelites to *seek the peace of the city where I have caused you to be carried away captives, and* **pray to the** LORD *for it: for in the peace thereof you shall have peace* (Jeremiah 29:7). This means they were to **pray for, and be a blessing to, their captors** who had destroyed their homes and their freedom! The Israelites, in turn, would be blessed in **answer to their prayers for restoration**. Through their painful years of captivity, the Israelites were conscious of the self-destructive results of hatred, of holding grudges, or of seeking revenge when one is mistreated or living under disagreeable circumstances.

This **basic principle of praying for our enemies** was illustrated by Stephen when he was being stoned to death. With the same hatred which had resulted in the crucifixion of Christ, the angry authorities dragged Stephen *out of the city, and stoned him....* (As he was dying, he) *cried* **(prayed)** *with a loud voice, Lord, lay not this sin to their charge* (Acts 7:57-60). Stephen could have avoided death by saying nothing, but he made it clear that the men of the council trying him were responsible for crucifying Jesus, *the Just One* (7:52). Stephen's faith and forgiving attitude in the face of death was the same as his Savior's attitude on the cross, and it surely must have made a powerful impression on those who witnessed Stephen's compassion toward his murderers. In the same spirit of love, we too need to **pray for those who despitefully treat us** (see Matthew 5:44). Those who seem to be our enemies today may someday be saved if we express the love of Christ to them as Stephen did to his persecuters.

When a Christian is loyal to Christ and living to please the Lord, the world will see a difference between his life and the lives of unbelievers.

Pity the people who, even though physically free, remain captive with dissatisfaction about their circumstances and are longing for a time when they can be free and enjoy living. Perhaps they are waiting until they have a promotion or a better home, or for retirement. But they are always waiting for release from their present situation. An even more pitiful example is the person who has been offended by the preacher and his sermon and has quit attending worship services. Often such people are engulfed in bitter resentment and have made themselves prisoners of their own miserable attitudes.

If we love someone, we want to be with that person and to know what pleases him or her since we desire to develop a lasting relationship. We also want to know what the person dislikes so that we can avoid displeasing him or her. Surely, these are important considerations in our relationship with our Lord. Why should God be attentive to our prayers if we are not interested in reading **His qualifications for acceptable prayer?**

We can't follow the Lord's commandments if we don't know how He wants us to live and what He wants us to do. However, we don't have to wait until we have read *all* the Bible before we start praying. Our spiritual level begins as "babes." Beginning there we are told to *desire the sincere milk of the Word, that we may grow thereby* (I Peter 2:2), and we will progress in our understanding of **the power of prayer**.

The Prophet Jeremiah exposed **the reason for Israel's unanswered prayers** and their continued confinement, saying: *The Word of the LORD is to them a reproach; they have no delight in it* (Jeremiah 6:10). The Lord further declared through His prophet: *I will bring evil upon this people . . . because they have not hearkened to My words, nor to My Law, but rejected it* (6:19). The Prophet Jeremiah, who knew well how to communicate with God, also reminds us: *I know that the way of man is not in himself: it is not in man that walks to direct his steps* (10:23).

The Lord also revealed to Jeremiah that, at a future time, He would make a new covenant *with the house of Israel . . . I will put My Law in their inward parts, and write it in their hearts; and will be their God, and they shall be My people* (31:33). The Lord's invitation to Jeremiah is also open to us: *Call* **(pray)** *to Me, and I will answer you, and show you great and mighty things* (33:3).

Do Christians today assume that, like the unsaved world, their own "good judgment" can take the place of the wisdom of our Creator? Without a doubt, God was heartbroken when He said to the Prophet Hosea: *There is no truth, nor mercy, nor knowledge of God in the land.* Consequently: *My people are destroyed for lack of knowledge: because you have rejected knowledge, I will also reject you . . . seeing you have forgotten the Law of your God, I will also forget your children* (Hosea 4:1,6).

Our faith in the Word of God can be measured by the influence it has on our conduct. How wonderful to know that, in the midst of the most difficult circumstances, we can rest assured that God is merciful and will protect and provide for the needs of His faithful servants!

Thought for the day: *Be kind one to another, tenderhearted, forgiving one another, even as God for Christ's sake has forgiven you* (Ephesians 4:32).

As the Cross of Christ is perfect
So my sins are washed away,
There God gave complete acceptance
To the sheep that went astray.

As the Power of Christ is perfect
— All authority to Him given —
So His strength will e'er sustain me
All the way from earth to Heaven.

Daniel Prayed

*S*oon after their capture, Daniel and other se-
lected Israelite prisoners of war were assigned new
names which would identify them as citizens of
Babylonia. This was an attempt by Nebuchadnezzar to remove the Israelites' identities as children
of God. The king's intent was that these select men
be taught to think and live like Babylonians.

The name Daniel means "God is my Judge," but
his Babylonian name Belteshazzar means "Prince
of Baal." As Daniel heard his new name called day
after day, it was intended to remind him that the
comfort, esteem, and high position he enjoyed in
his new society were all the result of his being the
"Prince of Baal."

*Nebuchadnezzar dreamed dreams, wherewith his
spirit was troubled. . . . The king commanded to call the
magicians, and the astrologers, and the sorcerers, and
the Chaldeans* (priestly class of Babylonians), *for to
show the king his dreams. . . . The Chaldeans answered
. . . the king, and said, There is not a man upon the earth
that can show the king's matter* (Daniel 2:1-2,10). Al-

though he was a captive slave, **Daniel prayed with his friends for God's mercies** that they not be killed with the wise men of Babylon. *The secret was revealed to Daniel in a night vision,* and he proclaimed to the king that *there is a God in heaven that reveals secrets, and makes known to the King what shall be in the latter days* (2:18-19,28).

The Lord gave miraculous wisdom to Daniel, and he interpreted the dream of Nebuchadnezzar, who then declared to the world that Daniel's God is the God of all gods. All these things happened because **Daniel and his friends prayed** (2:17-23,46-47).

Many years later, Belshazzar ruled Babylon near the end of the 70-year-long Jewish exile. Nebuchadnezzar is referred to three times as father of Belshazzar – meaning his ancestor (5:11,18). On the night that the Medo-Persian army invaded Babylon to defeat and execute Belshazzar, he was enjoying a great feast, celebrating with *a thousand of his lords. . . .* (using) *the golden vessels that were taken out of the Temple . . . at Jerusalem* (before Nebuchadnezzar destroyed it)*; and . . . drank in them. . . . and praised the gods of gold, and of silver* (5:1-4).

Suddenly the *fingers of a man's hand* (5:5) appeared and wrote on the wall. Belshazzar panicked *and his knees smote* (struck) *one against another* (5:6). His astrologers and soothsayers could not interpret the message on the wall. In desperation, Belshazzar summoned the aged Daniel, who boldly proclaimed: *This is the interpretation . . . God has numbered your kingdom, and finished it* (5:26). Pride often blinds the mind to the ways and will of God. That night the Medo-Persian army, led by *Darius . . . took the kingdom* (5:31).

Darius decided *to set over the kingdom a hundred and twenty princes, which should be over the whole kingdom; And over these three presidents; of whom Daniel was first.* Because of envy, the other presidents and princes conspired together and said to the king: *All . . . have consulted together to establish a royal statute . . . that whosoever shall ask a petition of any god or man for thirty days, save of* (except) *you , O king, he shall be cast into the den of lions* (6:1-2,7-8). Without realizing its real purpose or that Daniel had not been included in the *All,* the king signed the decree.

Now when Daniel knew that the writing was signed, he went into his house; and his windows being open in his chamber (room) *toward Jerusalem, he kneeled upon his knees three times a day, and prayed, and gave thanks before his God, as he did beforetime* (6:10). Consider that Daniel prayed at the risk of his life. He knew that if he continued praying to the living God, he would be thrown into the lions' den. God allowed him to be thrown to the lions, but Daniel was **saved from death because he prayed** and God closed the mouths of the lions. Daniel could have reasoned that, since he was not asked to worship an idol, why not cooperate *for thirty days* or just pray in secret? We need to ask ourselves: "If a similar decree were issued today, would it make a difference if we were told by government officials that we could not worship in our church on the Lord's Day for thirty days?" Yes, Daniel was cast into the den of lions, but afterwards he was able to testify to the king: *My God has sent His angel, and has shut the lions' mouths* (6:22). Because of his **faithful prayers**, God miraculously protected him.

Throughout his life, Daniel was a man of prayer and deeply concerned about the sins of Israel. In the first year of Darius' reign, Daniel understood the prophecy of Jeremiah regarding the 70 years Judah would be captive in Babylon. He then began to intercede greatly for Israel and recorded: *I set my face to the Lord God, **to seek by prayer and supplications, with*** *fasting, and sackcloth, and ashes: And **I prayed to the LORD my God**, and made my confession, and said, O Lord, the great and dreadful* (awesome) *God, keeping the covenant* (agreement) *and mercy to them that love Him, and to them that keep His Commandments; We have sinned, and have committed iniquity, and have done wickedly, and have rebelled, even by departing from Your precepts* (commands) *and from Your judgments: Neither have we hearkened to Your servants the prophets, which spoke in Your Name* (9:3-6).

Daniel's praying was much more than praying through a list of requests as some people do daily, even though daily prayer is admirable and needed. His prayer expresses **deep contrition, grieving, repentance, and confession**: *We have rebelled against God. . . . As it is written in the Law of Moses, all this evil is come upon us: yet made we not our prayer before the LORD our God, that we might turn from our iniquities, and understand Your truth. . . . Now therefore, O our **God, hear the prayer of Your servant**, and his supplications. . . . O Lord, forgive;, O Lord, hearken and do; **defer not, for Your own sake, O my God: for Your city and Your people are called by Your Name** (9:9, 13,17,19).*

Though he was not guilty of the nation's sins, he

identified with the sins of his people and pled for forgiveness – not because the people deserved it, but because they had violated the laws of God.

As with Daniel, there are times when an answer to prayer is crucial – a life or death situation when all else will be set aside. Then we will deny self and give Christ our undivided attention. Such self-denial often leads to fasting as an expression of our sincerity. It is as we pray and fast that we become more sensitive of the need to see God honored. Hopefully, we will be like David and will pray and fast *for Your city* (our nation) *and Your people who are called by Your Name* (Christians).

Why is it that some of our **most important prayers** never seem to get answered? Perhaps, among other things, we haven't been earnest enough to pray and fast as Jesus taught (see Matthew 6:16-18). Like Daniel's prayers, do ours **really represent a desperate concern**? This does not mean shouting louder, which could be merely the energy of the flesh. Rather, it means we should pray earnestly with a deep, heartfelt concern that is pleasing to God.

God has chosen **the prayer of faith, and often prayer and fasting, to release His power to answer our prayers**. Jesus said: *When you pray, you shall* *not be as the hypocrites* (self-righteous) *are: for they love to pray standing in the synagogues . . . that they may be seen of men. Verily* (Truly) *I say to you, They have their reward. But you, **when you pray, enter into your closet**, and when you have shut your door, pray to your Father which is in secret; and your Father which sees in secret shall reward you openly. But when you pray, use not vain* (meaningless) *repetitions, as the heathen do: for they think that they shall be heard for their much speaking* (6:5-7).

Jesus went on to say: **When you fast, be not, as the hypocrites**, *of a sad countenance: for they disfigure their faces, that they may appear to men to fast. Verily I say to you, They have their reward. But you, when you fast, anoint your head, and wash your face; That you appear not to men to fast, but to your Father who is in secret* (private)*: and **your Father**, who sees in secret, shall reward you openly* (6:16-18). **He didn't say "if" you fast, but "when" you fast. The Lord *expects* us to fast.** True, that means we will give up certain things – even "good" things – in order to give **time to be with the Lord in fasting and praying**.

If we are willing to seek the wisdom of God in His Word and **continue praying to please Him**, we can, like Daniel, make a difference in our world, for

God is *the same yesterday, and today, and for ever* (Hebrews 13:8).

Thought for the day: We know God is *able to do exceeding abundantly above all that we ask or think* (Ephesians 3:20).

No time, no time to study
To meditate and pray,
And yet much time for doing
In a fleshly, wordly way;
No time for things eternal,
But much for things of earth;
The things of little worth.
Some things, 'tis true, are needful,
But first things come first;
And what displaces God's own Word
Of God it shall be cursed.

Characteristics of
The Prayer Life of Christ

The prayer life of Jesus should have our undivided attention as we read the Scriptures that record His praying. **We need to take time each day** away from people and all activities, even from serving the Lord, **to devote to praying** and listening to what Jesus has to say as we read His prayer manual – the Bible. This was illustrated by two sisters, Mary and Martha. Martha was busy getting things ready for a dinner with their special guest Jesus while Mary sat at His feet and just listened to what He had to say. Jesus did not condemn Martha's activities, but He did say that Mary had chosen the *good part* (Luke 10:38-42).

God has placed in His only inspired Book the answers to all of life's problems. As we continue reading through the Bible and applying His truths to our lives, we become more like Him. Although thousands of years have passed since the Bible was written, it is just as relevant for us as it was for the early church. This is possible because human nature has not changed since the day Adam sinned.

Jesus' prayer life is first mentioned in the Bible in connection with His baptism. *Jesus . . . being baptized,* **and praying,** *the heaven was opened. And the Holy Spirit descended in a bodily shape like a dove upon Him, and a voice came from heaven, which said. You are My beloved Son; in You I am well pleased* (3:21-22). Prayer is power, and on this occasion, the heavens opened up, the Holy Spirit descended, and God spoke. This is indicative of what takes place in the spiritual realm when we pray.

It appears that **Jesus often devoted the early morning hours in prayer to His Father**. It is recorded that, *in the morning, rising up a great while* (very early) *before day* (while it was still dark), *He went out, and departed into a solitary* (deserted) *place, and there prayed* (Mark 1:35).

The day before this occasion was the Sabbath. Jesus had experienced a long and exhausting day's work, beginning in the synagogue in Capernaum where He was confronted with a man that had an unclean spirit. After casting out the demon, *His fame spread abroad throughout all the region round about Galilee. And forthwith* (at once), *when they were come out of the synagogue, they entered into the house of Simon and Andrew, with James and John. But Simon's wife's mother lay sick of a fever, and anon* (immediately) *they told Him of her. And He came and took her by the hand, and lifted her up; and immediately the fever left her, and she ministered to* (served) *them. And at evening, when the sun did set, they brought to Him all that were diseased, and them that were possessed with devils* (demons) (1:28-34).

Some of us probably would have felt we needed an extra hour's sleep the next morning or thought we were **just too busy serving the Lord to take time to pray**. But Jesus knew the importance of time away from a busy schedule to be with His Father.

On another occasion, *He withdrew Himself into the wilderness, and prayed* (Luke 5:16). Luke also tells us that Jesus' place of prayer was often on the Mount of Olives (see 22:39).

After Jesus appointed seventy men to go before Him to the places He would visit (see 10:1), they returned with amazing reports, saying: *Lord, even the devils* (demons) *are subject to us through Your Name* (10:17). Jesus replied: *Rejoice not, that the spirits are subject to you;* **but rather rejoice, because your names are written in heaven** (10:20). Knowing how important it is to thank God when He blesses our obedience, **Jesus prayed:** *I thank You, O Father, Lord of heaven and earth, that You have hidden these things from the wise and prudent, and have revealed them to babes: even so, Father; for so it seemed good in Your sight* (10:21).

Like the Apostles, we often lose sight of the eternal destiny of a life released from Satan's control and prepared for heaven. We are often so preoccupied with "our" successes and responsibilities that **we are tempted to tell people what we are doing** for the Lord **rather than what the Lord is doing** in and through us.

Prior to His arrest, Jesus said to Peter: *Simon, Simon, behold, Satan has desired to have you, that he may sift you as wheat: But **I have prayed for you**, that your faith fail not* (22:31-32). **He had prayed for Peter by name.** And even today, He is in heaven, interceding by name for each of us who prays (see Romans 8:34; Hebrews 7:25). And, finally, in the Garden of Gethsemane, Jesus said to His disciples: *Pray that you enter not into temptation. And He was withdrawn from them about a stone's cast, and **kneeled down and prayed**. . . . And being **in agony He prayed more earnestly**. . . . And when He rose up from prayer, and was come to His disciples, He found them sleeping* (Luke

22:40-41,44-45). Then He went to His sleeping disciples and, knowing they would soon face temptation, **He urged them also to pray** *lest you enter into temptation* (22:46). We learn from their experiences that our Lord never forces anyone to pray; He only tells us what is best. **Prayer is essential to keeping us from yielding to temptation.**

The indwelling Holy Spirit will strengthen us to withstand our trials and temptations when we pray. Jesus has promised believers: *I will pray the Father, and He shall give you another Comforter, that He may abide* (remain) *with you for ever* (John 14:16). We have not been left alone; we are *strengthened with might by His Spirit in the inner man* (Ephesians 3:16). With the assurance of the indwelling presence of the Holy Spirit, we can face life with certainty concerning our future. **Prayer enables us to enjoy a deep, inward peace** that *passes all understanding* (Philippians 4:7). His love and mercy empower us to overcome all prejudice, jealousy, hatred, and envy.

Jesus prayed before choosing the twelve apostles (see Luke 6:12-13) and He prayed again immediately preceding His transfiguration (9:29).

Before His crucifixion, Jesus knew that even His chosen Apostles would leave Him; but He loved them and forgave them. Never forget, Satan is *the accuser of our brethren* (Revelation 12:10); but it is comforting to know that Jesus sees far more in His followers than we see in ourselves or in each other. We often fail to permit Christ to rule our lives. But praise the Lord! We can say: "Though I'm not what I ought to be, I'm not what I used to be; and thanks to Christ, I'm becoming what I was intended to be."

As we regularly **take time each day to pray**, we should become more like Jesus. He prayed for each of us when He asked the Heavenly Father to *keep through Your own Name those whom You have given Me. . . . I have given them Your Word. . . . They are not of the world, even as I am not of the world. Sanctify* (Make holy for God's service) *them through Your truth: Your Word is Truth. . . . Neither pray I for these alone, but for them also which shall believe on Me through their word* (John 17:11,14,16-20).

Thought for the day: No opposition can rob us of the peace that God imparts when **we** *pray for them which despitefully use us* (Matthew 5:44; Luke 6:28).

Lord, Teach Us to Pray

After this manner therefore pray: Our Father which art in heaven, Hallowed be Thy Name. Thy Kingdom come. Thy will be done in earth, as it is in heaven. Give us this day our daily bread. And forgive us our debts, as we forgive our debtors. And lead us not into temptation, but deliver us from evil: For Thine is the Kingdom, and the power, and the glory, for ever. Amen (Matthew 6:9-13; see also Luke 11:2-4).

There was something about Jesus' praying that led His Apostles to realize that they needed to know more about how to pray. The Apostles never asked Jesus to teach them how to preach or teach; but, even though during their adult lifetime they had surely prayed every day, they now recognized their need to say: *Lord, teach us to pray* (Luke 11:1). Before He taught them how to pray, He first taught them "How **NOT to Pray**" when He said: *Hypocrites . . . love to pray standing in the synagogues . . . that they may be seen of men. . . . They have their reward. But when you pray,* (it should be as if you) *enter into your closet, and when you have shut your door* (as if no one else is present), *pray to your Father who . . . shall reward you openly* (Matthew 6:5-6).

Whenever **prayer** is offered to impress or inform someone other than God, it is hypocritical and pharisaical, and has no possibility of being answered. There may be one or even one hundred people who hear us **praying,** but that should not influence what we say since **prayer is speaking only to God** and never to anyone else.

Old Testament history reveals **many answers to prayer** from people of all walks of life to illustrate that **God does desire to answer our prayers.** And, if answers to prayer took place under the Old Covenant (Testament) – and they did – then Christians today can expect their prayers to be answered under the New Covenant because the *Holy Spirit . . . makes intercession for us, for we know not how to pray as we ought* (see Romans 8:26). Also, Jesus is now seated at the right hand of God to intercede in prayer for us day and night.

In seeking spiritual knowledge, there is no other source so exact and so complete as the Word of God. It is the only infallible Guide to answered prayer. As Christians, we have the Holy Spirit to help guide us *into all truth* (John 16:13). Our first step is to ask: *Lord, teach us to pray* (Luke 11:1), for none can teach like the Lord, who has revealed His instructions from Genesis through Revelation. *If . . . you shall seek the LORD your God you shall find Him, if you seek Him with all your heart and with all your soul* (Deuteronomy 4:29).

As **we study the prayers of God's people** in Scripture, we learn that they were heard, not because of impressive language, but because those who were **praying desired above all else to honor and exalt our Heavenly Father**.

While Jesus was on earth, He continually referred to or quoted the Old Testament to His critics apart from God's written Word. He was always revealing its true meaning, which many of them had replaced with "tradition" (see Mark 7:13).

In answer to His disciples' request: *Lord, teach us to pray,* Jesus gave no lofty, theological phrases. But, His answer may have surprised them, as well as Christians who do not pray every day. The **prayer** begins with *Our Father* . . . then moves to *His Kingdom* . . . and then to *His will,* all before there is any mention of their own needs.

Our natural impulse is to put self first by praying to our Heavenly Father to satisfy our needs. But the

Lord reveals that the reverse order is the way to pray effectively. Self-interests and secular influences can so darken our minds that we do not understand the true purpose that God has planned for our lives, and we fail to *seek first His kingdom and His righteousness* (Matthew 6:33). Although we have God's Word with its clear examples and sure promises, we might assume that since we have been Christians for many years we already know how to ask, without realizing that **we must meet certain conditions in order for prayer to be acceptable to God**. It cannot be emphasized too strongly that **every request in prayer should be to the glory of God**.

Some have asked: "Why is it necessary to express our needs to the Lord since He knows our desires before we pray?" Yes, He is already aware of our thoughts, and He knows our desires before we pray. Without a doubt, God knows all things. But He has committed His will to be accomplished through Christians praying to release the answers. God has chosen to accomplish His work in us *both to will and to do of His good pleasure* (Philippians 2:13).

For most Christians, taking time to pray is the most difficult of all spiritual responsibilities. We need always to remind ourselves that the order of priorities for our lives should be from God's point of view.

As we faithfully read the Bible with a desire – without reservation – to be all that He would have us be, as well as to do all that He would have us do, then His indwelling Holy Spirit enlightens our minds and stirs our hearts to **pray according to His will**. We need to be sensitive to the fact that as we read His Word, the Holy Spirit is available to provide the thoughts of what to **pray**.

King David wrote: *Evening, and morning, and at noon, I will pray, and cry aloud: and He shall hear my voice* (Psalm 55:17). Surely this is one of the reasons he was called a man after God's own heart (see I Samuel 13:14).

Time given to God helps us begin our day in a spirit of praise, gratitude, and conscious dependence upon Him. It also strengthens us to express His love to others throughout the day.

And at lunchtime, what a blessing to praise God for His goodness and thank Him for His provisions!

Then, in the evening hours, we can thank the Lord for His grace in keeping us and guarding us throughout the day. We can confess our failures and intercede for the needs of others – those near us, as well as the many spiritual needs throughout the world.

We should pray to the Father often during each day, regardless of how busy we are. On our way to work, at our jobs, or meeting with friends, we can be conscious of God and direct our silent prayers to Him. Let us ever be mindful that Jesus said: *Men ought always to pray, and not to faint* (give up) (Luke 18:1). And Paul admonished: *Pray without ceasing* (I Thessalonians 5:17).

We will never enjoy God's best blessings until we establish and practice a plan for **daily Bible reading and prayer**. There are no shortcuts to spiritual maturity.

Is any sick among you? let him call for the elders of the church; and let them pray over him, anointing him with oil in the Name of the Lord: And the prayer of faith shall save the sick, and the Lord shall raise him up; and if he have committed sins, they shall be forgiven him. . . . Elijah was a man subject to like passions as we are, and he prayed earnestly that it might not rain: and it rained not on the earth by the space of three years and six months. And he prayed again, and heaven gave rain, and the earth brought forth her fruit. Brethren, if any of you do err from the truth, and one convert him; Let him know, that he which converts the sinner from the error of his way shall save a soul from death, and shall hide a multitude of sins (James 5:14-20).

Thought for the day: *You, Lord, are good, and ready to forgive; and plenteous in mercy to all them that call upon You. Give ear, O LORD, to my prayer; and attend to the voice of my supplications* (requests). *In the day of my trouble I will call upon You: for You will answer me* (Psalm 86:5-7).

The ground of faith — God's Holy Word —
With which our lives are in accord
This Shield, no ill can penetrate
Nor Satan change its lasting state.

Thus glory comes to God each day
By exercising faith alway
Without which faith, we cannot please
The God who calls us to our knees.

Our Father in Heaven

And He said to them, When you pray, say, Our Father which art in heaven, Hallowed be Thy Name. Thy kingdom come. Thy will be done, as in heaven, so in earth (Luke 11:2).

The words *Our Father which art in heaven* are an introduction to all prayer. An understanding of God as our Father is basic to our relationship with Him. Our Creator demonstrates His love, compassion, and concern for us. Once we are born again, as part of the Body of Christ, we are always in His presence – and in His presence is the most powerful place to be for prayers that always prevail.

As Christians, our highest privilege is time alone in prayer and reading our prayer manual – the Word of God. When we read through the Bible, we listen to God; and in prayer, God our Father is listening to us. For 4000 years, no one addressed God as "Our Father." No one in the Old Testament could call the Creator "Our Father." Jesus made it possible for us to be born again of God: *As many as received Him, to them gave He power to become the sons of God, even to them that believe on His Name* (John 1:12-13). It is assuring to know that we are not talking to an indifferent Creator who is ready to knock us down when we make a mistake but to the One who invites us to call Him *Father* and who loves and cares for us (see Matthew 6:9).

We know that Jesus would not deceive His followers with a promise that He would not fulfill. And, in His Sermon on the Mount, He said: **Pray to your Father** *which is in secret; and your Father which sees in secret* **shall reward you openly** (6:6).

Although God created all mankind, not all people have chosen to be God's children. We all are descendants of Adam from whom we inherited a sin nature. Consequently, we were all *children of disobedience . . . and were by nature the children of wrath* (Ephesians 2:2-3). Even though the Pharisees were very religious, Jesus said to them: *You are of your father the devil* (John 8:44).

Because of our sinful nature, which separates us from the holy God, none of us qualifies to **pray to God as** *our Father* unless we first have been *born again* (3:3,7) into His family. The sinless Jesus made atonement for our sins by dying on the cross in our place (see II Corinthians 5:21). To accept God's gift of eternal life and have the privilege of calling Him *our Father*, we must pray for forgiveness of our sins and accept His Son, Jesus Christ, as our personal Savior. We then have the assurance that Jesus is now our *High Priest who can be touched with the feeling of our infirmities* (see Hebrews 4:15).

Multitudes of people pray daily to false gods, but Jesus said: *No man comes to the Father, but by Me* (John 14:6; see Matthew 7:21; John 3:5; 3:16; 6:37; Acts 4:12; Hebrews 4:14-16; 10:19-23; 11:6).

Jesus made this clear when He said to Nicodemus, who was a very religious man and teacher of the Old Testament Law: *Except a man be born again, he cannot see the Kingdom of God* (John 3:3).

Once a person receives Christ as Savior, he becomes a child of *our Father which art in heaven* and a joint-heir with Jesus Christ (see Romans 8:17), and is known as a Christian (see Acts 11:26; 26:28). As believers in Christ, we are then under our loving Heavenly Father's protective care and provision.

Jesus assures us that **we can approach our Father in prayer without fear**, just as children approach their earthly father, knowing that he loves them.

*Beloved, **if** our heart condemn us not, **then** we have confidence toward God. **And whatsoever we ask, we***

receive of Him, because we keep His Command-
ments, *and do those things that are pleasing in His sight*
(I John 3:21-22).

And this is the confidence that we have in Him, that,
if we ask (pray for) *any thing according to His will,*
He hears us (5:14). Since *we know that He hears us,*
whatsoever we ask, we know that we have the
petitions that we desired of Him (5:15).

If we pray for a need and do not receive a specific
answer, then there may be **something wrong about**
either the prayer or the one offering the prayer. It
may be that *we ask, and receive not, because we ask*
amiss, that we may consume it upon our lusts (James
4:3). Or, it could be because we do not *do those things*
that are pleasing in His sight. But, sometimes the answer is "wait" as it was with Abraham and Sarah for
so many years before God answered their prayer for
a son. So, we must not accept Satan's condemnation
if our prayers aren't answered immediately. Let us
not seek to excuse the unanswered prayer until we
have read the Bible and observed the character of
the people whose prayers God chose to record.

It is far easier to examine ourselves (see I Corinthians 13:5) or to excuse the unanswered prayer
than it is to search for biblical qualifications that

bring about answers to prayer.

It's also much easier to pray in generalities than to pray specifically. But "general" prayers get "general" answers because of failure to be specific.

There are other times when the answer is a refusal, as when Paul prayed three times that God would remove his *thorn in the flesh*. Paul did receive the Lord's answer to that prayer, although it was not what he asked for. God did not leave His servant in uncertainty as to His will; He let Paul know that His *grace was sufficient* to compensate for his suffering (II Corinthians 12:7-9).

It is His delight when we pray according to His will, and the only way to know His will is through His Word. It is a fact that *the sacrifice of the wicked is an abomination to the* Lord: *but **the prayer of the upright is His delight*** (Proverbs 15:8).

God loves us – not because we are perfect but because He is our Father. He is never partial and He *is no respecter of persons* (Acts 10:34). This means that in His infinite love, patience, long-suffering and wisdom, He reaches down to each one of us and tenderly provides for our needs without discrimination.

Even though *our Father knows what things we*

have need of, before we ask Him (Matthew 6:8), in order to receive those *things*, our Father in heaven has given us the responsibility to release them by praying in the Name of Jesus. We are to **pray only to** *our Father who gives good things* (what is good for us) *to them that ask Him* (7:11).

The Lord revealed through Paul that we do not know how to pray as we ought (see Romans 8:26). We can be so thankful that the indwelling Holy Spirit will move upon our hearts to realize what our true needs are and will intercede for us. And we have the utmost confidence that *Our Father . . . in heaven* will respond to our requests (prayers) as soon as it is in our best interest to do so.

The Christian who refuses to be obedient to his Heavenly Father may presume that, regardless of where he goes or what he does, he will always obtain an answer to his prayer, but he will surely be disappointed.

As Christians, we have already received the Holy Spirit, but we still need to ask and pray earnestly for Christ's Spirit to take control of our lives. In our earthly walk, the flesh will constantly war against the spiritual, and it is up to us to submit to the Holy Spirit.

Thought for the day: *Quench not the Spirit* (I Thessalonians 5:19).

What shall it profit any man
This whole wide world to gain
If, at the ending of life's span
Nothing but guilt remain.

How different, then, the true-born son
Of God — to whom is given
The fulness of Christ's victory won —
On earth, as well as Heaven.

Seek first the Kingdom of thy Lord,
All blessing shall accrue;
God's favor, says His holy Word,
Will surely come to you.

So, rest in Him, poor weary heart,
His all-sufficient grace
To thee each day He will impart
Until you see His face.

Hallowed Be Thy Name

*H*allowed be Thy Name (Luke 11:2) means: May the Name of God be held holy, honored, and revered. "Holy" is an essential characteristic of God in the Old Testament and defines one of the attributes of the Only True God. It means He is without sin of any kind. Because He is holy (absolute perfection), Christians cannot attain "absolute perfection" such as God. Jesus said: *If any man will come after Me, let him deny himself, and take up his cross daily, and follow Me* (9:23). A Christian is wholly dedicated to living for Jesus as explained by Peter: *As obedient children, not fashioning* (conforming) *yourselves according to the former lusts in your ignorance: But as He which has called you is holy, so be you holy in all manner of conversation* (behavior); *Because it is written, Be holy: for I am holy* (I Peter 1:13-16).

The more importance we place on the Almighty God, His Name, His will, and His Kingdom in comparison to our earthly concerns, the more powerful our prayers will be. *For of Him, and through Him, and to Him, are all things: to whom be glory for ever. Amen*

(Romans 11:36).

Jesus taught: *Whatsoever you shall ask in My Name, that will I do, that the Father may be glorified* (honored) *in the Son. If you shall ask any thing in My Name, I will do it. If you love Me, keep My Commandments* (John 14:13-15). *Verily, I say to you, Whatsoever you shall ask the Father in My Name, He will give it you. Until now you have asked nothing in My Name: ask, and you shall receive, that your joy may be full . . . ask in My Name* (16:23-26).

The phrase *ask in My Name* means that Christians may come before the Father in prayer as Jesus' representatives, for we now live under His authority as *ambassadors for Christ* (II Corinthians 5:20). It is not who *we* are, but who *He* is that makes it possible for us to pray in Jesus' Name.

When our Lord ascended to heaven, He gave His Name as the key to receiving all we need in order to conduct His business. This is illustrated by a bride that becomes united to her bridegroom. She gives up her name to be called by his name and has the full right to use it. She may purchase in his name and he counts on her to care for his interests. They are now one (see Genesis 2:24). The heavenly Bridegroom does the same.

To pray or act in the name of another person implies that we have his or her authority to do so. When Jesus told us to ask in His Name, He gave us the legal right to approach God the Father using all the authority, power, and excellence inherent in Jesus Himself. We do not need to draw back from our Creator like the people did who were delivered from Egypt and who, in fear of God, asked Moses to pray for them. The Israelites often asked the prophets to pray for them. But Christians have the privilege of calling God *our Father*. We can go directly to Him in the authority and righteousness of Christ. *For He* (God) *has made Him* (Christ) *to be sin for us, who* (Christ) *knew no sin; that we might be made the righteousness of God in Him* (II Corinthians 5:21).

Everything depends on our relationship to our Holy God. The power that Jesus' Name has in our lives is the power it will have in our prayers. When Christ rules in all areas of our lives and our desire is for Him to be glorified (see 10:5), then we will have power in prayer. It is not only what we pray for but what we have become through Christ that makes our prayers acceptable to God the Father.

As a child of the King, our desire should be to uphold His sacred Name and His Kingdom before all else, and His will should be our daily desire. The true child of God desires to live for His honor and His glory and His coming Kingdom, all of which give us reason to praise Him.

Jesus taught His disciples to pray: *Hallowed be Thy Name* (the Holy One revered above all else). God is our Father; but using the personal title "our Father" must not lessen our devotion and reverence for Him. There will never be any spiritual depth in prayer power until we recognize that the God of Creation is holy and His Name is to be *Hallowed*.

Some Christians are thoughtlessly speaking the Name of the Lord in an unholy way – taking His Name in vain in trivial conversation by saying such things as: "Oh, Lord, this," or "Oh, my God," or by using His precious Name in bitterness and anger. Many talk foolishly about God by ignorantly referring to Him as a kindly old grandfather or "the Man upstairs." What an insult to use His Name in such ways as these instead of recognizing God for who He is in holy, reverent prayer and praise! **We can't expect our Father to answer our prayers** if we are using His Name in vain.

We are reminded: *Be not rash with your mouth, and let not your heart be hasty to utter anything before*

God: for God is in heaven, and you upon earth: therefore let your words be few (Ecclesiastes 5:2).

Jesus said: *Every idle word that men shall speak, they shall give account thereof in the day of judgment* (Matthew 12:36).

If our prayers are to be answered, we must desire, above all else, that our words and our prayers honor and glorify the Lord. This begins when we are conscious of our littleness and His greatness. *Let us lift up our heart with our hands to God in the heavens* (Lamentations 3:41).

Honoring the Lord is an important principle of effective prayer. This is illustrated in the Scriptures where Moses prayed that God would not destroy the Israelites in the wilderness, even though they deserved to be destroyed! Moses' chief concern was not for Israel but for the honor of the One True God. Moses pleaded with God that if He turned against His own people whom He had delivered from Egypt, the heathen nations would assume that He was not powerful enough to lead His people into the promised land. (See Exodus 32:11-13.)

Consider our prayers for our national security against terrorism. Do we pray that God will protect our nation, but fail to **pray that our citizens will**

repent of their immorality and honor the God of Creation by restoring the Bible, prayer, and the Ten Commandments to our schools and in public places? God alone has made it possible for the United States to be the greatest nation on earth. But, our sins may soon result in our nation's destruction.

Our needs should always be subordinate to the Father's Kingdom and His will in our lives: *As in heaven, so in earth* (Luke 11:2).

Thought for the day: The believer's desire should always be to *seek first* (Matthew 6:33) the will of God in our prayers.

Dear Lord, through Christ, I come to Thee
Claiming His Blood to cover me.
To cleanse from every doubt and sin
My Entrance to the Court within.

Oh! Christ of God, in Thee I joy
With joy that Thou alone canst give,
Do Thou my being all employ
That to Thy glory I may live.

Thy Kingdom Come

*O*ur Heavenly Father's only begotten Son Jesus is the King of the greatest Kingdom on earth. And, as children of the King and *joint heirs with Christ* (Romans 8:17) of His Kingdom, it is our delight to pray: *Thy Kingdom come. Thy will be done* (Matthew 6:10; Luke 11:2). We are not praying that God will get control of things. Some have imagined that the natural laws of the universe, governments, and people, as well as Satan, are presently beyond God's control. But God has always been in full control and rules over everything every day, including every world ruler. God has revealed this in His Word, saying: *By Me kings reign. . . . even all the judges of the earth* (Proverbs 8:15-16). *The king's heart is in the hand of the* Lord, *as the rivers of water: He turns it wherever He will* (21:1). *He removes kings, and sets up kings* (Daniel 2:21). He is even in control of Satan. In the book of Job we read: *And the* Lord *said to Satan, Behold, all that he* (Job) *has is in your power; only upon himself put not forth your hand* (Job 1:12). God permitted Satan to take away Job's possessions and his health; but

He didn't permit him to take Job's life.

When Jesus said to **pray**: *Thy Kingdom come. Thy will be done in earth,* He expects all who have received Jesus as Savior and Lord to **pray** that others will receive Him as Savior and Lord. His Kingdom will continue to spread *into all the world* (Mark 16:15).

In the parable of the sower, Jesus said: *The good seed are the children of the Kingdom* (Matthew 13:38). And Jesus spoke of being *born again* (converted) as the qualification to enter the Kingdom of God (John 3:3,5). Soon the King of kings will *send forth His angels to gather out of His Kingdom all things that offend, and all who do iniquity* (Matthew 13:41). Not many seem to realize that **the unrighteous shall not inherit the Kingdom of God.** *Be not deceived: neither fornicators, nor idolaters, nor adulterers, nor effeminate, nor abusers of themselves with mankind, Nor thieves, nor covetous, nor drunkards, nor revilers, nor extortioners, shall inherit the Kingdom of God* (I Corinthians 6:9-10; see also Galatians 5:17-21).

We praise the Lord that the Holy Spirit did not have the Apostle Paul stop after listing sins that will keep many people from entering heaven. He had him continue to write concerning those who have repented and been delivered from sinful habits: *And such were some of you: but you are washed, but you are sanctified* (set apart), *but you are justified in the Name of the Lord Jesus* (I Corinthians 6:11).

However, we are by nature self-centered; consequently, our prayer requests are often for self. But, **if our prayers are to be effective, the desires of God must occupy the central place** in our lives. This is God's purpose in creating us and is our purpose for living. *For you are bought with a price: therefore glorify God in your body, and in your spirit, which are God's* (I Corinthians 6:20). When we *seek first His Kingdom and His righteousness,* He has assured us that our daily needs *will be added to us* (Matthew 6:33). God *has translated* (transferred) *us into the Kingdom of His dear Son: In whom we have redemption through His blood, even the forgiveness of sins* (Colossians 1:13-14). We are to **pray for *laborers*** to advance His Kingdom as Jesus said: *Pray therefore the Lord of the harvest, that He will send forth laborers into His harvest* (Matthew 9:38). He also declared: *This Gospel of the Kingdom shall be preached in all the world for a witness to all nations; and then shall the end come* (24:14).

All who sincerely pray: *Thy Kingdom come* will take seriously our Lord's command to *go . . . teach all nations . . . to observe all things whatsoever I have com-*

manded you (28:19-20). We should be greatly concerned that people in every nation of the world have God's Word and through-the-Bible teaching literature to help them *observe all things* in order to fulfill the Great Commission. As Christians, we have **a responsibility to pray and to help evangelize the world**. But, not many Christians can actually be missionaries in some far-off country. However, all of us – young or old, rich or poor – can **pray; and through our united prayers**, missionaries and mission ministries throughout the world can be empowered to overcome the forces of evil.

The Apostle Peter wrote: *You are . . . a peculiar* (special) *people* (God's own purchased possession); *that you should show forth the praises of Him who has called you out of darkness into His marvelous light* (I Peter 2:9). When Peter said we are *a peculiar people*, he was not implying that we are odd but that we are a chosen people – chosen to share in the glorious and compassionate ministry of Christ, who came *to seek and to save that which was lost* (Luke 19:10). Christ is saying: "I have chosen you as a key person to pray: *Thy Kingdom come*." This should become our greatest desire above all earthly needs.

When we pray: ***Thy Kingdom come***, we are an-

163

ticipating a literal kingdom with Christ ruling earth just as He does in heaven. This present system of world governments will soon be destroyed, and Christ will return to earth as King of kings to rule the world as promised (see Revelation 19:11-16).

We have the privilege of fulfilling Christ's command to *be witnesses for Him . . . to the uttermost part of the earth* (Acts 1:8).

Thought for the day: All the world needs to hear the Good News that *the kingdoms of this world will become the kingdoms of our Lord, and of His Christ; and He shall reign for ever and ever* (Revelation 11:15).

God is our Refuge and our Strength
In every time of need.
If life — throughout its breadth and length —
His Spirit e'er doth lead.

His Angels, ministering spirits are
Encamped around His own —
To guard from dangers, near and far;
— We never are left alone.

Thy Will Be Done

*I*n much of our prayer life, our minds are not focused on God's will, but on what we want from Him. Jesus taught that before mentioning our own needs or desires, we should first pray: *Hallowed* (held in reverence and submissive to) *be Thy Name. Thy Kingdom come. Thy Will Be Done, as in heaven, so in earth* (Luke 11:2). **One of the purposes of prayer is to bring our wills into conformity to His *will being done*** in our lives.

When we pray: *Thy will be done,* we should mean: "Lord, I want Your will above my own will. I need to know and accept Your Word to live the way You want me to live."

As we read **God's Word**, it not only **prepares us for prayer**, but it enables us **to pray according to His revealed will**. We can be so grateful that the Lord has given us His Word to enable us to know what His will is. We're told in I John 5:14-15: *And this is the confidence that we have in Him, that, if we ask any thing according to His will, He hears us: And if we know that He hears us, whatsoever we ask, we know that we* *have the petitions that we desired of Him.*

The great men of faith recognized that accomplishing the Lord's will was dependent on their obedience to His Word. If His Word was a command, they simply obeyed. Consider Abraham: *So Abram departed, as the LORD had spoken to him* (Genesis 12:4). Think of Moses, who led the Israelites out of Egypt, and also of Joshua, who led them to conquer Canaan: *As the LORD **commanded Moses** his servant, **so did Moses** command Joshua, **and so did Joshua;** he left nothing undone of all that the LORD commanded Moses* (Joshua 11:15). The Apostle Paul, whom God used to write the majority of our New Testament, said: *I was not disobedient to the heavenly vision* (Acts 26:19). When God spoke, these men of God were obedient; and **when they prayed according to His will, God answered their prayers.**

God expects no less of us today, and we can expect no less from Him. *Beloved, if our heart condemn us not, then have we confidence toward God. And whatsoever we ask, we receive of Him, because we keep His Commandments, and do those things that are pleasing in His sight* (I John 3:21-22).

Consider the far-reaching effects of having our wills in harmony with God's will. How wonderful to know that we, through **our prayers and gifts**, enable others to discover the true treasures of life eternal!

We become partners with Christ in prayer and co-workers with Him in helping others throughout the world to discover His will for their lives. The majority of the world worship false gods and do not know that God created us and provided a guide for us to live by.

The Bible contains the best news in all the world. It is the one and only inspired message from heaven and reveals how to receive the best out of life. No other guide on earth can compare to the Bible because it reveals God's will for our success, happiness, and peace of mind. As you **read your Bible (Guide) each day**, pray: *Open . . . my eyes, that I may behold wondrous things out of Your Law* (Psalm 119:18).

Jesus left no room for doubt when He said: *I am The Way, The Truth, and The Life: no man comes to the Father, but by Me* (John 14:6). Christ came to earth to die for our sins. His work of salvation was recorded in His Word in order that it might be shared with others throughout the ages so that all nations may be reached with the Good News, *and then shall the end come* (Matthew 24:14).

His command to His disciples was, and still is: *Pray therefore the Lord of the harvest, that He would send forth laborers into His harvest* (Luke 10:2). **Our prayers are vital** in accomplishing the work and ministry He gave us to do.

In His high-priestly prayer, Jesus used two ordinary words – *work* and *word*. He fulfilled His responsibility and prayed: *I have finished **the work**. . . . I have given them **Your Word*** (John 17:4,14).

Our submission to Christ will make us willing to live so that others may also know and believe that *the Son of man is come to seek and to save that which was lost* (Luke 19:10).

There has never been a time in history when we could more effectively reach millions of people in every nation of the world. God has given us in the free world both the freedom and the ability – through the printed page, radio, satellite, the internet, and other means of communication – to effectively reach every nation with Bibles so they may know what it means to pray: *Thy will be done.*

Thought for the day: May each of us pray daily: *Thy will be done* – that the Lord's eternal purpose may be accomplished in and through our lives.

Give Us This Day Our Daily Bread

*J*esus taught us to pray for *our daily bread* (Matthew 6:11). The Greek words *daily bread* are not found anywhere in the Bible except in this prayer: *Give us day by day our daily bread. . . . If a son shall ask bread of any of you that is a father, will he give him a stone? or if he ask a fish, will he for a fish give him a serpent?* (Matthew 6:9-13; Luke 11:3,11). *Daily bread* implies prayer for all our material necessities as well as **prayer for our spiritual food** – *the true Bread from heaven. . . . is He which comes down from heaven, and gives life to the world* (John 6:32-33). Jesus used the words *daily bread* to let us know He is the supplier of ALL our needs. We have been assured that *God shall supply all our needs according to His riches in glory by Christ Jesus* (Philippians 4:19).

This does not mean that we are to do nothing but pray for His provisions and expect God to provide every material thing we want and every spiritual thing we need without our full participation

169

and cooperation. **God is expecting us to pray** and to do everything we can to provide for our needs while we fully depend on His guidance and strength. He illustrated this with Joshua's conquest of the promised land. Three times God said: *The land which I do give them* (Joshua 1:2,3,6). Did this promise mean that, as the Israelites approached, the Canaanites would flee or disappear and the Israelites would assume possession of the "free gift of God"? The fact is, they had to fight for every foot of ground and conquer it as God provided the strength and guidance to possess it. The key to their conquest is clear: *This Book of the Law shall not depart out of your mouth but you shall meditate therein day and night, that you may observe to do according to all that is written therein: for then you shall make your way prosperous, and then you shall have good success* (1:8).

We too should have the utmost confidence that, as *we observe to do according to all that is written therein: then we shall make our way prosperous, and then we shall have good success.*

There will be times such as the Apostle Paul experienced when he wrote: *I have learned, in whatsoever state I am, therewith to be content. I know how to be abased* (made low), *and I know how to abound* (have abundance) ... *to be full and ... to suffer need. I can do all things through Christ who strengthens me* (Philippians 4:11-13).

Jesus is that *Bread ... that comes down from heaven* (John 6:33), for He is *the Word made flesh* (1:1-14). **We need to pray** that, as we daily read the Word of God, **His spiritual Bread will become our way of life**.

The words *daily bread* also express all our personal needs – material, emotional, social, spiritual, and financial. Our Lord said that a man's life *does not consist of the abundance of things that he possesses* (see 12:15). Paul also wrote to Timothy: *Having food and raiment let us be ... content* (I Timothy 6:8). But, we are by nature too concerned about what we want to wear, what we need to eat, and how we can secure our future welfare. Jesus had already said that we should pray: *Give us day by day our daily bread* and assured us that **He will answer our prayers**. If we *seek first His Kingdom* (Matthew 6:33), we have our priorities straight.

Jesus cautioned that we are to *take no thought* (be not anxious) *for our life, what we shall eat; neither for the body, what we shall put on* (see Luke 12:22). *(For after all these things do the Gentiles* (the secular world) *seek: for our Heavenly Father knows that we have need of all these things. But seek . . . first the Kingdom of God, and His righteousness; and all these things* (physical needs) *shall be added to us* (Matthew 6:31-33; Luke 12:30-31).

We need day by day to take in *our* (spiritual) *daily bread* so it will nourish and strengthen us to overcome the giants of jealousy, greed, hate, lust, envy, unbelief, and fear. Peter instructed the early Church: *As newborn babes, desire the sincere milk of the Word, that you may grow thereby* (I Peter 2:2). *Newborn babes,* although totally helpless, express no fear about what they shall eat or what they shall wear. This illustrates how we are to trust *our Heavenly Father, who knows that we have need of all these things.*

Is not the life more than meat (our daily necessities), *and the body than raiment* (clothing and shelter)? *Behold* (observe) *the fowls of the air: for they sow not, neither do they reap, nor gather into barns; yet our Heavenly Father feeds them. Are you* (His children) *not much better* (more valuable) *than they* (mere common birds)? (Matthew 6:25-26).

Having been *born again* into His Kingdom (John 3:3), our highest purpose should be *the Kingdom of God and His righteousness.* Once, as the crowds gathered around Jesus, a woman spoke up and said how blessed was the woman who gave birth to Him. And Jesus replied: *Rather, blessed* (divinely favored) ***are they that hear the Word of God, and keep it*** (Luke 11:27-28).

In our prayers, we are to consider others' needs, as well as our own. Notice that Jesus didn't tell us to pray: "Give ME this day what I want." **A prayer that produces results** is not a selfish prayer. Jesus said we are to pray: *Give US . . . OUR daily bread.*

Something special happens to us when we can sincerely **pray for the needs of others**, whether they are in our neighborhood or in far off places such as Africa or India. We have made progress in our spiritual maturity when we begin to see things from God's perspective and not from our own limited personal interests. We should **truly pray that God would open our eyes to see the needs of others as He sees them** and that our hearts would be broken with the things that break His heart.

God has provided prayer as a link to release His power for us to accomplish His will as revealed in His Word. It bridges all distance. The moment we pray according to His will in the Name of Jesus, we can touch the lives of people in any country in the world and know that He will answer.

It is important that we remember the Lord's request that we pray for laborers – laborers who will give and **laborers who will pray** – that every person in every nation be provided with the true Bread from Heaven (see 10:2; John 6:32). *How shall they believe in Him of whom they have not heard? and how shall they hear without a preacher?* (Romans 10: 13-14). No one in the world is more starved than a person who doesn't have a Bible, for they are dying an eternal death, and many of them do not realize it.

Physical hunger is far less important than the spiritual hunger that exists in the people who are lost. Just as the natural body hungers for physical food, a Christian hungers for truly satisfying spiritual food from God's Word. Sadly, many people of the world attempt to satisfy that hunger with "food" from other sources, such as astrology, or the many false religions; but these things can never satisfy the hunger to know the True Eternal God.

Thought for the day: *If you then, being evil, know how to give good gifts to your children: how much more shall your Heavenly Father give the Holy Spirit to them that ask Him?* (Luke 11:13).

Forgive Us Our Sins

We are invited to pray for forgiveness only on the condition that *we also forgive every one* (Luke 11:4).

Jesus then warned: *If you forgive not men their trespasses* (sins), *neither will your Father forgive your trespasses* (sins) (Matthew 6:15). Lest it be overlooked, on another occasion the same statement is plainly given by Jesus: **When you stand praying, forgive, if you have anything against any**: *that your Father also which is in heaven may forgive you your trespasses. But **if you do not forgive, neither will your Father which is in heaven forgive your trespasses** (Mark 11:25-26). **If we are to expect** forgiveness for our sins and enjoy daily fellowship with God and receive **answers to our prayers**, then we must forgive all who have sinned against us, regardless of how serious their sins were.

Most of us don't find it difficult to say: "Father, I've done wrong. Forgive me." But we often find it difficult to pray the necessary other half of this prayer: "I hold no grudge, hard feelings, ill will, hatred, or evil plans of retaliation toward anyone who has wronged me."

It seems normal to stand up for our rights – to fight back against those who treat us unjustly, to get even by inflicting suffering upon anyone who offends us, and to be delighted when they suffer and seem to reap what we think they deserve. However, it is a serious **hindrance to answered prayer** to harbor an unforgiving attitude and have a desire to bring about an offender's downfall. God has warned: *Rejoice not when your enemy falls, and let not your heart be glad when he stumbles: Lest the LORD see it, and it displease Him, and He turn away His wrath from him* (Proverbs 24:17-18).

Unforgiving attitudes or hatred not only **keep our prayers from being answered**; they also keep our sins from being forgiven (see Matthew 18:21-35). Bitterness, revenge, or ill will toward anyone is self-destructive and indicates that we are not being controlled by the Holy Spirit. To illustrate our need for His guidance, we read: *Be not drunk with* (under the control of) *wine, wherein is excess; but be filled with* (controlled by) *the Spirit* (Ephesians 5:18). Furthermore, having a bitter, unforgiving spirit indicates that we are not living nearly as close to Christ as we should.

No one is justified in taking revenge; we are not qualified to be judge, jury, or executioner. We dare not assume the position of God, who had Paul write: *Dearly beloved, avenge not yourselves, but rather give place to wrath* (opportunity for God's wrath): *for it is written, Vengeance is Mine; I will repay, says the Lord* (Romans 12:19; see also Deuteronomy 32:35; Psalm 135:14; Hebrews 10:30).

If we are unjustly treated, we should pray for our offender. All thoughts of revenge are temptations from Satan to weaken our relationship with Christ; but, the indwelling Holy Spirit can enable the Christian to be merciful and forgiving rather than hateful toward an offender.

Our response of mercy, longsuffering, and love to the unkind behavior of an offender reveals that we are controlled by the Holy Spirit rather than by our old sinful nature (see Romans 8:1-9).

To forgive is to care more about a person than about what he has done. This is illustrated in Jesus' parable about the father who welcomed home his prodigal son who had wasted his father's wealth. He prepared a great feast for him and in every way restored him. He cared more about his son than about the huge loss of possessions that his son had wasted (see Luke 15:11-32). Forgiving love releases the offender without obligating him to pay for his offense in any way. This is how God loves us and why He has forgiven and restored us to Himself.

Just as we make daily requests for food and all our other needs, we need to **daily pray:** *Forgive us* **as** *we also forgive every one* (see Matthew 6:12). And, as we thank God for His immeasurable forgiveness, we need also daily to praise Him that *as far as the east is from the west, so far has He removed our transgressions from us* (Psalm 103:12).

Anyone who comes to Christ as a repentant sinner and trusts in Him to forgive his sins will be forgiven. *You, being dead in your sins and the uncircumcision of your flesh, has He* (God) *quickened* (made alive) *together with Him* (Jesus), *having forgiven you all trespasses* (Colossians 2:13).

We are to forgive others with the same sincerity with which we expect our Heavenly Father to forgive us.

All Christians are called to a ministry of reconciliation. We are to forgive and restore relationships as if offenses had never happened.

To illustrate how necessary it is to forgive, Jesus told about a king who had a servant who owed him ten thousand talents – an amount far beyond the servant's ability to pay in a lifetime. He begged for mercy and the lord of that servant had compassion and forgave him. But that same servant went to a fellow servant who owed him a small amount, took him by the throat, and demanded immediate payment. Despite his fellow servant's pleading, he had him thrown into prison until he should pay the debt. (See Matthew 18:23-30.)

When the king heard this, he was angry because the one whom the king had forgiven so much did not express similar compassion to his fellow servant. Therefore, the king *delivered him* (the unforgiving servant) *to the tormentors, till he should pay all that was due to him.* And Jesus said: *So likewise shall My Heavenly Father do also to you, if you from your hearts forgive not every one his brother their trespasses* (sins, offenses) (18:34-35).

Thought for the day: We are to regard everyone, without exception, as a person created in the image of God, one for whom Jesus died to save. *Let us not love in word, neither in tongue* (talk); *but in deed* (action) *and in truth* (I John 3:18).

Lead Us Not into Temptation; But Deliver Us from Evil

*T*his last petition may seem to infer that God is the one who tempts us to sin. However, God is just and holy and *cannot be tempted with* (by) *evil, neither tempts He any man: But every man is tempted, when he is drawn away of his own lust, and enticed* (James 1:13-14). Knowing how easy it is to misjudge and often fall far short of our expectations to live a holy life, we can pray with all sincerity and urgency: *Lead us not into temptation; but deliver us from evil* (Luke 11:4). We are powerless by human strength to withstand the deceptions of the evil one (Satan).

It is through prayer and the power of the indwelling Word of God that we are able to recognize, avoid, and overcome temptation. Jesus warned His disciples: **Watch and pray, that you enter not into temptation:** *the spirit indeed is willing, but the flesh* (human nature) *is weak* (Matthew 26:41).

When we **pray:** *Lead us not into temptation*, we are reminded that *there has no temptation taken you* *but such as is common to man: but God is faithful, who will not suffer* (permit) *you to be tempted above that you are able; but will with the temptation also make a way to escape, that you may be able to bear it* (I Corinthians 10:13).

Temptations come to all of us. Even Jesus was tempted at least three times by Satan during His 40-day fast in the wilderness. He defeated Satan by quoting Scripture each time He was tempted (see Matthew 4:3-10); thus He demonstrated for us how to be victorious over sin and Satan.

Having learned that we cannot trust our good intentions, we realize how much more we need to pray: *Lead us not into temptation.* Trials and testings often expose the fact that there was not as much real desire to live for Christ as we had assumed. Or, perhaps after yielding to a temptation we realize how self-centered and self-reliant we really are.

Satan never ceases in his efforts to lead us astray, to discourage or defeat us; he is always *seeking whom he may devour* (I Peter 5:8). We should sincerely **pray to our Heavenly Father that the indwelling Holy Spirit** will keep us from yielding to temptation. When we neglect to read God's Word, we ignore the source of our strength and wisdom.

Prayer is not to be an isolated act used only when we are caught up in a situation that we cannot resolve. It needs to be a daily, vital part of our lives. Jesus described it as asking, as seeking, and as knocking (see Matthew 7:7) – an ascending scale of earnestness.

How wonderful it would be if we would realize the importance of always *trusting in the Lord with all our hearts; and lean not to our own understanding. In all our ways acknowledge Him, and He will direct our paths* (Proverbs 3:5-6). Through His Word, the guidance of the Holy Spirit, and **our prayers, God is able to deliver us from temptation** when we are tempted to sin. He can, and will, *make a way to escape* when we have a sincere desire to live to please our Heavenly Father.

Temptation is always deceptive, and Satan will always suggest that we yield "just this once" or "just one more time." We dare not trust in our own wisdom or strength. Instead, we need to **pray as the psalmist did**: *Keep back Your servant . . . from presumptuous sins; let them not have dominion over me* (Psalm 19:13).

Each day we need to pray: *Lead us not into temptation*, not merely when we may think we can't cope with our situation. And *deliver us from evil* should remind us of our personal weakness against the powers of Satan and prompt us to **pray daily for deliverance** from the evil one.

Before Peter was tested, on the night he denied the Lord, he boasted that he would never forsake Jesus even if everyone else denied Him. Peter went so far as to say he would even die for Him (see Matthew 26:33-35). Peter had to learn that his boasting was foolish self-confidence.

Jesus knew that Peter was so self-confident that he would ignore His command to pray. So, He let Peter know that he would deny Him three times: *But I have prayed for you, that your faith fail not* (Luke 22:31-32). We should understand from this statement that Peter could have had victory that night **if he had prayed as Jesus had said**.

One reason for the scriptural accounts of temptation and sin in the lives of some of God's people is to warn us against self-confidence and of the necessity to pray (see I Corinthians 10:11).

In order to withstand the devil, we are admonished to *put on the whole armor of God,* which directs us to the Word of God as the source of wisdom and power to overcome the devil's deceptions (Ephesians 6:11-13). *And take the . . . Sword of the Spirit, which is the Word of God: Praying always with all prayer and supplication in the Spirit, and watching thereunto with all perseverance and supplication for all saints* (6:17-18). The whole armor, including the girdle, breastplate, shoes, shield, and helmet, is defensive and protects the body of the Christian. The only weapons of offense against the enemy are **the Sword of the Spirit, which is the Word of God** and *praying always . . . with all perseverance.* As we put on the armor and take up these weapons of offense, we are assured of being *more than conquerors* (over all the enemy's temptations) *through Him that loved us* (Romans 8:37).

Thought for the day: Praise God that Jesus knows what we are experiencing when we are tempted, for He *was in all points tempted like as we are, yet without sin. Let us therefore come boldly to the throne of grace* **(and pray)***, that we may obtain mercy, and find grace to help in time of need* (Hebrews 4:15-16).

For Thine Is The Kingdom

The concluding words of Jesus' blueprint for prayer are: *For Thine is the kingdom, and the power, and the glory for ever. Amen* (Matthew 6:13).

This declaration is in perfect harmony with other Scriptures, such as: *Yours, O Lord, is the greatness, and the power, and the glory, and the victory, and the majesty: for all that is in the heaven and in the earth is Yours; Yours is the kingdom, O Lord, and You are exalted as head above all* (I Chronicles 29:11). How thrilling it is to know that *the angels stand round about the throne, and about the elders and the four beasts, and fall before the throne on their faces, and worship God, Saying, Amen: Blessing, and glory, and wisdom, and thanksgiving, and honor, and power, and might, be to our God for ever and ever. Amen* (Revelation 7:11-12)!

All Christians can surely shout in thankful agreement with King David and the King of kings, as well as the angels in heaven, glorifying our Creator and praying: *For Thine is the Kingdom, and the power, and the glory for ever. Amen* (So be it)!

Each of the phrases in The Lord's Prayer reveals basic **requirements Jesus gave to make our prayers acceptable to God**. As we pray according to His instructions, we'll be **assured of answers to all our prayers**.

As we meditate on the *power and the glory* of God's Kingdom and His will being done *for ever*, we have an overwhelming desire to join the psalmist, who invites the faithful to *come, **let us sing** to the* LORD: ***let us make a joyful noise** to the Rock of our salvation.... O come, **let us worship** and bow down: **let us kneel before the** LORD **our Maker**. For He is our God; and we are the people of His pasture, and the sheep of His hand* (Psalm 95:1,6-7).We have an overwhelming desire to express **heartfelt gratitude and thanksgiving** for the privilege of uniting with heaven in praising our Father. We want the world to know that there is no greater joy than allowing His will to be done in our lives.

Praise and prayer will lift our thoughts above the level of our material needs to the higher plane of adoration as we glorify the Heavenly Father, our precious Savior Jesus Christ, and the indwelling Holy Spirit.

Some people lack spiritual fulfillment because

they have chosen to reflect the mood and attitude of unbelievers when confronted with adverse circumstances, such as the loss of a job, the death of a loved one, a divorce, the betrayal of a friend, or some other painful experience. They have chosen to be fearful, unhappy, and dissatisfied. They deprive themselves of **answered prayer, and** *the peace of God, which passes all understanding* (Philippians 4:7). The Christian who knows that God is in control has made the choice to live by faith, regardless of circumstances, and to sincerely pray: *Thy will be done.... For Thine is the Kingdom, and the power, and the glory, for ever. Amen* (Matthew 6:10-13). As our thoughts dwell on how wonderful our Lord is, how can we even consider yielding to the temptation to complain and find fault!

When we think of **all our Lord has done for us, in us, and with us in answer to our prayers, and all He has promised to us** for all eternity, we will *serve the* LORD *with gladness* and *come before His presence with singing* (Psalm 100:2). Our *gladness* will be in direct proportion to our desire that His *will be done.*

Thought for the day: *The* LORD *is good; His mercy is everlasting . . . His truth endures to all generations*

(100:5).

Editor's Note: The concluding phrase in The Lord's Prayer (see Matthew 6:13) has been in the English King James Version of the Bible for almost 400 years, as well as in all earlier manuscripts that were available at that time.

However, they are not found in some more-recently-discovered ancient manuscripts of the Bible. For this reason some contemporary Bible versions omit the words or place them in small print in the margin.

We do not hesitate to believe that Jesus expects this marvelous phrase: *For Thine is the kingdom, and the power, and the glory for ever. Amen* to remain as the inspired Word of God and to be a vital part of our prayers, since they exalt our Heavenly Father. They in no way diminish or contradict the truth of the rest of Scripture; but rather, complement and confirm it.

We prefer to believe that the Holy Spirit led Jesus to say: *Man shall not live by bread alone, but by* ***every Word that proceeds from the mouth of God*** (Matthew 4:4); and ***every Word*** would include the Lord's sacred prayer: *For Thine is the Kingdom, and* *the power, and the glory for ever. Amen* (6:13). We have chosen not to question the integrity of Matthew 4:4 or the Apostle Paul who wrote that *All Scripture is given by inspiration of God* (II Timothy 3:16).

We cannot believe that the Almighty Creator would have allowed numerous errors that were not inspired to exist as the Word of God for 400 years. Isn't it more reasonable to believe that the Creator who controls the universe led the translators to the exact manuscripts that confirmed what He inspired men to write? *For ever, O LORD, Your Word is settled in heaven* (Psalm 119:89). As for God, His way is perfect. He is in control, and we do not believe He made a mistake. We believe that *all* of The Lord's Prayer *was given by inspiration of God and is profitable . . . that the man of God may be perfect* (complete, well prepared), *thoroughly furnished to all good work* (II Timothy 3:16-17).

Intercessory Prayer
Luke 11:5-8

*O*nly God can provide the real needs of the human heart, but He has chosen **His faithful servants to accomplish His will**. Jesus illustrates this by a parable, saying: *Which of you shall have a friend, and shall go to him at midnight, and say to him, Friend, lend me three loaves; For a friend of mine . . . is come to me* (hungry), *and I have nothing to set before him* (no food to give him)*? And he from within shall answer and say, Trouble me not: the door is now shut, and my children are with me in bed; I cannot rise and give you. I say to you, Though he will not rise and give him, because he is his friend, yet because of his importunity* (persistence in making his request) *he will rise and give him as many as he needs. And I say to you, Ask, and it shall be given you; seek, and you shall find; knock, and it shall be opened to you* (Luke 11:5-9).

Our attention is drawn to a man who wanted to help someone in need: *A friend is come to me.* Then, a confession: *I have nothing.* Then the unexpected re-

190

fusal: *I cannot* (will not) *rise and give you.*

This parable illustrates **the importance of the intercessory prayer of someone who** *has nothing* **but desires to meet the need of one less fortunate**.

First, our attention is given to the love which seeks to help the needy around us. As he continued to plead with his friend for food to satisfy his unexpected guest, we are encouraged to hear that he would **receive** *as many as he needs*.

We are given the wonderful assurance that, **as he kept on asking, he received**, because he refused to give up (quit praying). **The reward of continued prayer is never meager.** Jesus said: *He will . . . give him as many as he needs*.

This parable also reveals the friendship we have with God. As a true friend of God, we confirm that relationship by being a friend to the needy. The friendship of God to us and our friendship to others go hand-in-hand. **God is always more desirous to help the needy than we are, and He works through our prayers** and necessary efforts to do so.

A biblical illustration of this principle is given when **Abraham prayed for Lot** to be spared from destruction in Sodom when Lot deserved nothing but the judgment of God (see Genesis 18:23-33; 19:

1-30). **Moses also prayed** for the children of Israel when *the L*ORD *said to Moses, I have seen this people, and, behold, it is a stiffnecked* (rebellious, stubborn) *people: Now therefore let Me alone, that My wrath may . . . consume* (destroy) *them: and I will make of you a great nation. And Moses besought* (prayed to) *the L*ORD *his God . . . . Turn from Your fierce wrath . . . . Remember Abraham, Isaac, and Israel, Your servants, to whom You swore* (promised) *. . . and said to them, I will multiply your seed* (descendants) *as the stars of heaven . . . . And the L*ORD *repented* (relented) *of the evil* (harm) *which He thought to do to His people* (Exodus 32:9-14). **Samuel prayed** and the Israelites were saved when they were attacked by the Philistines at Mizpeh (I Samuel 7:8-13). After a 3½-year drought, **Elijah on Mount Carmel prayed** for the people to receive rain *and there was great rain* (I Kings 18:42-45).

Just as men of God, in times past, demonstrated that **the power of God was released when they prayed for others**, we too can experience answers to our prayers for others.

When we draw near to God as a friend of the poor, the sinner, and the lost, we can count on His response: *For every one that asks receives; and he that seeks finds; and to him that knocks it shall be opened*

192

(Luke 11:10).

Friendship depends upon conduct, for Jesus said: *You are My friends, if you do whatsoever I command you* (John 15:14). We also read: *Faith without works is dead. . . . (but) by works was faith made perfect. And the Scripture was fulfilled which says, Abraham believed God . . . and he was called the Friend of God* (James 2:20-23). It is as such a *Friend of God* that we can go to Him even at midnight – even when it is inconvenient for us – seeking to help another. And, when we ask according to His will, we can be assured that He will hear our request **and answer our prayers**.

Our Father always looks at **the motive behind . our prayers**. If what we ask is merely for our own self-esteem, we should not expect the desired answers; but, if we truly desire that our Lord be glorified in the answer, we can expect a favorable answer. *Whatsoever you do, do all to the glory of God* (I Corinthians 10:31). Our motives will always be tested. Just how real is our concern for the needy? Will we sacrifice our time, even when it is inconvenient, and continue going to the Lord in prayer until we have obtained from the Father all that is needed for another?

The person we help or intercede for may or may not appreciate or deserve the kindness shown. Our responsibility, however, is not to the person who needs our help but to the Lord, who is the true Owner of all creation, and who provides the opportunities for us to express His love.

We should be exceedingly grateful that Jesus Christ **intercedes in prayer on our behalf**! Because He is God, He knows all things. *For by Him were all things created, that are in heaven, and that are in earth, visible and invisible, whether they be thrones, or dominions, or principalities, or powers: all things were created by Him, and for Him: And He is before all things, and by Him all things consist* (hold together) (Colossians 1: 16-17). Thus, **He always knows how to pray for our best interests**. *Christ . . . who is even at the right hand of God . . . also makes intercession for us* (Romans 8:34).

Thought for the day: *Wherefore He is able also to save them to the uttermost* (completely) *that come to God by Him, seeing He forever lives to make intercession for them* (Hebrews 7:25).

His Elect . . .
Cry (Pray) Day and Night

*Jesus spoke a parable to them to this end, that men ought **always to pray, and not to faint** (lose heart and give up); Saying, There was in a city a judge, which feared not God, neither regarded (nor respected) man: And there was a widow in that city; and she came to him, saying, Avenge me (Give me justice; Defend me) of mine adversary (opposer). And he would not for a while: but afterward he said within himself, Though I fear (revere) not God, nor regard man; Yet because this widow troubles me, I will avenge her, lest by her continual coming she weary me. And the Lord said, Hear what the unjust (unrighteous) judge says. And shall not God avenge His own elect, which **cry (pray) day and night to Him**, though He bear long with them? I tell you that He will avenge them speedily* (Luke 18:1-8).

This parable illustrates the importance of continued urgent prayer for our personal needs. The Lord leads us to see the inability of this poor widow to provide for her needs. She was asking the administrator who was assigned to provide them but he showed no compassion.

Perhaps Jesus gave this parable on being **persistent in prayer** because it's so easy to give up and assume it isn't the will of God if He doesn't answer when expected. Some are prone to "leave it in the hands of the Lord" without further praying about it. But, the fact is, Jesus, our Intercessor, has given us the **responsibility to continue praying** when we know our prayers are according to the will of God and, therefore, will glorify Him.

Jesus is revealing **the importance of continuing to pray** for what we need even when it seems that God will not answer our prayer.

This points out how foolish it is to assume that, if there is no answer the first time we pray for something, we should stop praying.

We must do all we can — not merely "leave it up to the Lord." The person who is assured of the Lord's will knows: "**Never give up praying while waiting for an answer.**" You can expect an answer, *for He is faithful that promised* (Hebrews 10:23).

Jesus tested the faith of a Gentile woman when He *departed into the coasts* (districts) *of Tyre and Sidon. And, behold, a woman of Canaan came out of the same coasts, and cried to Him, saying, Have mercy on me, O Lord, You Son of David; my daughter is grievously vexed with a devil* (miserably afflicted). *But He answered her not a word* (no answer to her prayer). *And His disciples came and besought* (urged) *Him to send her away; for she cried after them. But He answered and said, I am not sent but* (except) *to the lost sheep of the house of Israel. Then she came and worshiped* (bowed before) *Him, saying, Lord, help me. But He answered and said, It is not meet* (fitting) *to take the children's* (Israel's) *bread, and to cast it to dogs* (Gentiles). *And she replied, Truth, Lord: yet the dogs eat of the crumbs which fall from their masters' table. Then Jesus answered and said to her, O woman, great is your faith: be it* (the answer to your prayer) *even as you will. And her daughter was made whole* (healed) *that very hour* (Matthew 15:21-28).

It may seem that Jesus was rude to this desperate Gentile lady, since to call someone a "dog" in that society was the greatest of insults. But she wasn't offended, for she knew from whom she was asking.

All prayers are not immediately answered. There are many reasons why we can expect delays in answer to our prayers. One of these reasons is that *we wrestle not against flesh and blood, but against princi-*

palities, *against powers, against the rulers of the darkness of this world, against spiritual wickedness in high places* (Ephesians 6:12; see also Daniel 10:12-13). But we keep on praying!

Thought for the day: Our Heavenly Father always knows what is best for His children. *Delight yourself . . . in the LORD; and He shall give you the desires of your heart* (Psalm 37:4).

Does thy sacrifice seem useless
As you humbly serve the Lord?
Yes, to one who is most faithless
And ignores His Holy Word.

But to one who really knows Him
And His mighty Word of power
Nothing his sight of faith can dim
Even in the trying hour.

Nothing lost in any service
Rendered to our gracious Lord
Whether it seem glad or grievous
There will be a full reward.

Jesus' Prayer Life
(Chosen Selections)

*T*he four Gospels record more than 50 references concerning the prayer life of our Lord during His brief stay on earth.

If your desire is to be like Jesus in conduct as well as conversation, you will read and re-read all of His prayer manual that we call the Bible. It was given by God to let mankind know how to live and how to communicate with our Creator. The Bible gives clear instructions for Christians who want definite answers to prayer.

Examples of the fundamentals of effective praying can be seen in the 250 prayers that are recorded in the Bible. The Christian who wants the best in life will also observe Jesus' prayer life and pray for what He prayed: *Whatsoever you ask in My Name, that will I do, that the Father may be glorified* (John 14:13). *I pray . . . for them which you have given Me. . . . that they also may be one in Us. . . . that the love wherewith You have loved Me may be in them, and I in them* (17:9,21,26). And He asked us to *pray the Lord of the harvest, that He will send forth laborers into His harvest* (Matthew 9:38).

In the midst of crowds pressing to hear Him, it was important for Him to have time to be alone with His Father in prayer. With His life in us, we have the same need for times of separation from all activities, even serving the Lord, to be alone with the Father in prayer. If our prayer life is to be effective, it will often require the sacrifice of sleep, business, and time with friends. Christ is our example. If He needed to give valuable time in prayer, how much more we too must be alone with the Father if we desire answers to our prayers.

Luke emphasizes the life of Jesus as a **Man** like ourselves except He was without sin. Consequently, the Gospel of Luke records more instances of Jesus' prayer life than were recorded in all three of the other Gospels combined.

The first mention of Jesus praying was following His baptism. Luke adds: *And praying, the heaven was opened. And the Holy Spirit descended . . . and a voice came from heaven, which said, You are My beloved Son: in You I am well pleased* (Prayer is power and our Father responded) (Luke 3:21-22).

Matthew records that *He departed . . . into a desert*

place apart: and when the people had heard thereof, they followed Him on foot out of the cities. And Jesus.... saw a great multitude, and was **moved with compassion** toward them, and He healed their sick. And when it was evening.... Jesus said to them, They need not depart; give them to eat. And they said to Him, We have but five loaves, and two fishes.... And He commanded the multitude to sit down on the grass, and took the five loaves, and the two fishes, and **looking up to heaven, He blessed (prayed), and broke**, and gave the loaves to His disciples, and the disciples to the multitude (Matthew 14: 13-19). This event is a reminder that **at every meal we too should pray and bless the Lord for what He has provided**.

Following this, *He went up into a mountain **apart to pray**: and when the evening was come, **He was there alone*** (14:23). On another occasion while alone **praying, *His disciples were with Him*** (see Luke 9:18).

Mark records that after a confrontation in Capernaum with demons that He had cast out of a man, and after He had healed Peter's wife's mother, then *all the city was gathered together. . . . And He healed many that were sick . . . and cast out many devils. . . . And in the morning, rising up **a great while before day, He went out, and departed into a solitary*** *place, and there prayed* (Mark 1:33-35).

After Jesus healed a leper, *great multitudes came together to hear, and to be healed by Him of their infirmities. And* **He withdrew Himself into the wilderness, and prayed** (Luke 5:15-16). His life was far more exhausting than what any of us realize. Yet, with our pressing personal and business duties and our giving priority to opportunities to serve the Lord, we too need to schedule times of prayer.

In a synagogue where Jesus taught, *there was a man whose right hand was withered* (6:6); and Jesus healed him (see 6:7). And the scribes and Pharisees *were filled with madness; and communed one with another what they might do to* (destroy) *Jesus. And it came to pass in those days, that* **He went out into a mountain to pray, and continued all night in prayer to God** (6:11-12).

In Caesarea near Mount Hermon, *He* (Jesus) *was alone praying, His disciples were with Him: and He asked them, saying, Whom say people that I am? . . . Peter answering said, The Christ of God. . . . And He said to them all, If any man will come after Me, let him deny himself, and take up his cross daily, and follow Me. . . . After these sayings* (words)*, He took Peter and John and James, and went up into a mountain to pray. And as He*

*prayed, the fashion of His countenance was altered. . . .
And there came a voice out of the cloud, saying, This is
My beloved Son: hear Him* (9:18,20,23,28-29,35).

*And it came to pass, that, as **He was praying** in a
certain place, when He ceased* (praying), *one of His
disciples said to Him, Lord, teach us to pray* (11:1-2).

In one of the four instances of vocal prayer, John
recorded Jesus' prayer: ***Father, I thank You that You
heard Me. And I knew that You hear Me always****: but
because of the people which stand by I said it, that they
may believe that You have sent me* (John 11:41-42).

Near the end of His ministry, Jesus said: *Now is
My soul troubled; and what shall I say? Father, save Me
from this hour. . . . Father, glorify Your Name.* Immediately after Jesus prayed, *then came there a voice from
heaven, saying, I have both glorified it, and will glorify
it again* (12:27-28).

In the large upper room in Jerusalem, *He took the
cup, and gave thanks. . . . **And He prayed, took bread,
and gave thanks*** (Luke 22:17,19). Jesus told His disciples: ***I have prayed for you, that your faith fail not***
(22:32). He had been praying for Peter by name.

He was alone with His disciples after He had
finished His earthly ministry. *Jesus lifted up His
eyes to heaven, and said, Father, the hour is come. . . .*

this is life eternal, that they might know You the only true God, and Jesus Christ, whom You have sent. I have glorified (honored) *You on the earth. I have finished the work which You gave Me to do. . . . I have manifested* (made known) *Your Name to the men which You gave Me . . . and they have kept Your Word* (John 17:1,3-6). All true believers should unite in glorifying the *Father* and Christ our Lord, and in keeping His Word.

The difference between the weakest of Jesus' disciples and the wisest worldly, unsaved person is revealed as Jesus continued His prayer to His Father in heaven: **I have given to them the words which You gave Me;** *and they have received them, and have known surely that I came out from You, and they have believed that You did send Me* (17:8). Notice the order: *The words which You gave Me, I have given to them,* and **they have received them**. This underscores that *faith comes by hearing, and hearing by the Word of God* (Romans 10:17).

Jesus also prayed to the Heavenly Father: *Keep through Your own Name those whom You have given Me* (John 17:11). Jesus continued praying for all who would believe on Him, *that they may be one, even as We* (God the Father, God the Son, and God the Holy Spirit) *are One* (17:20-22). How comforting to know that His prayer included every Christian as He prayed: *I have given them Your Word. . . . They are not of the world, even as I am not of the world. Sanctify* (Keep holy for God's service) *them through Your truth: Your Word is Truth. . . . Neither pray I for these alone, but for them also which shall believe on Me through their word* (17:14,16-20).

Following this most holy prayer, we are brought within the sacred precincts of Gethsemane Garden, one of our Lord's favorite places to pray. Jesus and the eleven disciples were alone. Jesus knew that Judas would soon arrive with the religious leaders who would lead the hostile mob and the Roman military to crucify Him. His disciples did not grasp the exceeding importance of what Jesus then said: ***Pray that you enter not into temptation*** (Luke 22:40). They could not imagine a reason to be tempted while in their favorite place to pray, so they relaxed and slept. *And He was withdrawn from them about a stone's cast, and kneeled down, and prayed. . . . And being in an agony **He prayed more earnestly**. . . . And when He rose up from prayer, and was come to His disciples, He found them sleeping for sorrow, And said to them, Why sleep you? rise and pray, lest you enter into temptation* (22:41,44-46). This was His last recorded prayer before He was crucified. Just moments later, all of Jesus' apostles yielded to temptation and forsook Him.

Satan is the *accuser of our brethren* (Revelation 12:10), but it is comforting to know that Jesus sees far more in His followers than we see in ourselves or in each other. He knew His disciples would leave Him and that Peter would use bad language to emphatically deny that he even knew Jesus; but Jesus loved them and forgave them.

His final prayer on earth was spoken while on the cross. Three of His final statements were prayers. Luke tells us that after the soldiers had nailed Him to the cross, He said: *Father, forgive them; for they know not what they do* (Luke 23:33-34).

*It is Christ that died, yea rather, that is risen again, who is even at the right hand of God, **who also makes intercession for us*** (Romans 8:34; see Hebrews 7:25). Our prayers are vital for the Lord to use us in fulfilling His will.

He is waiting for us to pray. We can pray while driving down the road or ironing a shirt or working in a machine shop; we can be letting the Lord use us to release His blessings through our prayers to meet needs anywhere in the world.

Thought for the day: *Until now you have asked nothing in My Name* (authority)*: **ask (pray), and you shall receive**, that your joy may be full* (John 16:24).

Make me an intercessor —
One who can really pray —
One of the Lord's remembrancers
More strong in faith each day.

Make me an intercessor
Through whom the Spirit pleads
For sin and sorrow on every side,
For others' desperate needs.

Make me an intercessor
In ardent love for Thee
Who commands to pray and not to faint
Till faith brings victory.